The Galactic Council

Book 1

Copyright © 2015, Robbie Mackenzie
All rights reserved. No part of this book may be reproduced, stored, or transmitted by any means — whether auditory, graphic, mechanical, or electronic — without written permission of both publisher and author, except in the case of brief excerpts used in critical articles and reviews. Unauthorized reproduction of any part of this work is illegal and is punishable by law.

Front cover image courtesy of the Hubble space telescope.

www.imetatron.com

We welcome you. We are the Galactic Council. We are a group of beings who preside over the Council that has many members from all over the Universe. Every group of members that is in the Galactic Council are at the point of their evolution where they have expanded their consciousness and contribute consciously to the affairs of the Universe. And embrace the many different Galactic civilisations both physically and within their deep conscious states.

As you move forward through this book your awareness will expand. We recommend, before you go any further that you first read 'This is the Clarion call' and 'This is the Healing book' by Metatron. To be ready for these concepts and benefit from these words you must prepare yourselves. This is a book like no other. As a species you have evolved over many thousands of years and we have been watching you with great interest. As you evolve into your divine selves we see much compassion in you. We see much diversity and humour and we have enjoyed observing you greatly. It is only now as the Worldwide quarantine on your Planet is lifted that we are able to contact you on a more obvious level. You have only reached this point very recently and we are pleased that this can now be a two-way communication.

We have great fondness for the different diverse cultures on your Planet and we see you getting ready to become one as a Planet. As you open up your telepathic communication and you recognise how to use your vessels properly, all wars will subside. Do not fear anything dear ones. In this ascension process it is very simple and you have been given all the tools that you need. You must relax and expand your minds if you are to benefit from this book.

There is much ridicule from the people who really understand your potential. This is merely a control system that is trying to keep you down and out of your magnificent selves. Do not be in any fear. None of this need be preached to anyone, it merely needs to be lived. For as these concepts all open up you will be in so much bliss you will not care about what other people think. And your light will shine so brightly that none of the effects of the lower chakras will be able to take hold. And the positive energy will bring you to connection with all the other beings on your Planet that are making great changes. The Earth paradigm is ready to change. You are ready to come together. We see much love. All the old systems are failing. All the control systems are breaking down; you are coming into your power.

Your divine selves are eternal and this is the most exciting time that you have experienced on your Planet.

We thank you for your open mindedness. We thank you for your interest. We thank you for your love. We are the Galactic Council. You are ready for this message.

Be at peace.

I am the Channel that Spirit used to bring this information down. It has been my great honour and privilege to be a part of this project.

I developed as a medium in a meditation circle years ago. I didn't know about ascension or any of the New Age stuff before I developed, but I always felt that there was something else in life that I should be doing.

Since learning how to channel, my life has become much better, and I am often astounded by the stuff that comes out. The process is simple - I go into a meditative state and I feel a great loving presence and hear a phrase repeated over and over. As soon as I hear the phrase, I let it repeat a few times so I know it is not just my inner dialogue, and then repeat it. After that I just keep on talking and sometimes can still be talking half an hour later.

This is all recorded and afterwards I transcribe it. This whole book was written this way, and it has been wonderful to feel the bliss that the high vibration brings. I have learned a lot from this whole process and my life is much better for it. I hope that reading this book brings you as much joy and understanding as it has done for me.

Best wishes,

Robbie Mackenzie

We come to you from Orion. Many of the Star Seeds on your Planet are from here. Although you are seeded with many different beings from many different places that are incarnated in Human bodies, you consider Aliens to be from other Planets, extra terrestrials. However there are many different consciousnesses that are walking around with your Human bodies that are from many different places in the Universe, many different places in the Galaxy and many different dimensions. Many of the beings reading this will have epiphany moments and realize that they are Star Seeds themselves. But you are also from this Planet. As your physical incarnation is here you have been divinely placed to shine your light. You are here to raise the vibration, raise the consciousness, raise the awareness and open up your Merkabas, open up your light and open up all your diverse powers. Once you have followed instructions fully there will be nothing that will stop you in your lives from showing others the way to live from a higher vibrational place. Your manifestations will be instant.

Your communications are already expanding and your technological awareness is becoming much more advanced. There is a lot that has been shielded from you. For there are many vessels that have crashed on your Earth plane and much of your modern age has been reverse engineered. There have also been voluntary contributions from many different places in the Galaxy. As you recognize what has been around you for millennia and you recognize that you are already in communication with many Star Seeds and through many different walk ins that are giving out this information, your Planets resources are going to be used in a fair, open and collectivized manner as you recognize your own power.

Breathe in these statements. Fully assimilate them into your consciousness and we will move on.

I am Bashanthi Mayawar. It is the closest interpretation I can give you of my name, for we are translating through this being into your English language. We chose English for this book because it is the language that has evolved mostly on your planet, but that's root seeds come from the language of light. It is my honor and privilege to take you through the steps of opening your understanding to what you can achieve, as you become full members of the Galactic Council. As newbie's here you may feel very overwhelmed as you did at the beginning of your school days. But very soon you understood the routine of this new world of schooling and you came to an understanding of your place within this system. Unlike your Human schools, the hierarchical system does not wish to take any energy from you, ridicule you or self aggrandize. All new members have great wisdom in their innocence and we honor this wisdom.

The oldest members of the Galactic Council are trillions of years old. Their civilizations are honored greatly for how they have benefitted the Universe. These beings have evolved past the need for skulls and their brains have swelled so large their heads are as large in diameter as their bodies. They have such a complete telekinetic command over their surroundings that no one can get within ten thousand light years of them without them being able to affect their vessels. They are who you think you understand as the Annunaki. This is the closest interpretation we can give you of their names and they are purely benevolent beings. They have evolved past the need for conflict of any kind. Their bliss radiates out to the Universe. Just one of these beings has the mental processing power of all seven billion people on your Planet and there are many of these beings. They are here to help you open up to your initiations and expand your mental awareness and your power and communicate with you. These are the most revered members of the Galactic Council. Symbolically they wash your feet. They shall now give you a telepathic initiation, which will ready you for the rest of this book. Expanding your mental body that you may transcend all obstacles.

Sit in a quiet position.

Visualize your crown chakra opening up.

Be open to receive this.

As the sightings increase on your planet you will become less and less incredulous as a species about the existence of extra terrestrial life. We are being very sensitive to your people. We are being very sensitive to the whole of humanity for we do not wish to spread any fear. We do not wish to cause any anxiety. There is enough anxiety and fear on your Earth plane already without us adding to it. We are here to lift you up; we are here to expand your awareness so that you might seek contact more and more. Of your greatest channels that are fully open, not all have had first contact. But this will happen more and more. We are connecting with you on deeper levels so that you may be open and willing to accept the truth of the Universe. Over the last century there has been many different sightings and much contact telepathically. We have been inspiring your works of Art, we have been inspiring your Films, we have been inspiring your books, and we have been inspiring your science fiction. Truly we look forward to you opening to the next level of our communication. When you focus on the higher aspects of your lives you come closer to being able to travel the Universe physically. We have much greater technology than you can ever imagine. We had your level of technology billions of years ago and you are already exploring the Universe so the more and more you come to these concepts the easier it will be. Do not fear anything, the time has come.

As your synchronicities increase with your lives, your vibration raises, everything will be transformed and life will never be the same again once you connect fully, telepathically to your star family. We are expanding the light for you all.

As you expand your awareness you will recognize the polarized effects on the Earth plane. More and more people are diving deeply into duality and all the lessons that can be learned from this are being learned very intensely. You are coming to a place where your consciousness is ready; your consciousness is opening up. The more and more that open up, that open their merkaba, that connect with their higher selves, that connect with all the beings that are surrounding the Earth right now, and there are millions of beings, the more the collective consciousness is affected in a positive way. The tide has already turned; the positive is transforming the world.

We are here to give you the opportunity to have first contact. The more you connect telepathically, the quicker it will be for you to connect physically. As a species you are ready and this next stage is the most exciting time your World has ever seen. These channeling's are important. You taking them on board and fully assimilating them will lead to more and more synchronicities for you to see the World as it really is. And for you to detach from the lower energies, the lessons that you have learned in past incarnations and the lessons that you do not need to learn anymore. We are helping with all this.

There are ships stationed around every part of the Globe. There are beings inside the Earth that have their bases on Mother Earth also. **You are not the only inhabitants of this planet**. The work that has been done has been benevolent to further your species and you are ready to travel the Galaxy now. Ready to meet the many species that love you and have been observing you. You will be urged to travel to sacred sights; you will have a longing to connect with individuals of a higher vibration and you will connect more and more. The more and more that you connect, the easier it will be. For the more conversations you have about the expanded universe in respect without ridicule, the easier this transition will be.

More and more curiosity is happening and more and more want **the truth.** For this Planet has been used for profit. Not by the majority of your species but by the ones who keep this idea down. The ones who suppress this are the ones who have a vested interest in you remaining ignorant and keeping the knowledge from you. But the more open you become to recognizing that you are moving forward to being a Galactic race of travelers physically, the more the excitement will build and the more you will take the time to develop your own selves. For it is within your vessel, within your consciousness and your opening aura, connecting to your higher self, your guides and the beings that have been watching you and helping you that you will make the transition from telepathic connection to physical connection. And the less shocking it will be when our ships land. When it is an accepted and obvious fact to your species.

Understand that we have nothing to fear from you. We do not fear your War. Our technology is far more advanced than you can ever imagine. We have nothing to fear in this way. We do not want to scare you. Your weapons are primitive to the many cultures that are helping your society. We have no worries in that regard. We wish to make this an easy transition for you, for when you come to this understanding and you trust us we will share with you the wonders of the Universe. It is time for you to experience this. Within this localized Galaxy, Earth is the most eagerly watched. We are excited to join with you. Your hearts are opening.

You are at the dawn of a new era. We are ready to give you the information you need. We have been preparing the different sacred sites.

The great Pyramid of Giza - is the most significant point on your Earth plane. It is a reminder of your merkabas and is a very powerful place. There are many ships stationed above the great pyramid and it was a Galactic base for many eons. The pyramid that is there is not the first pyramid that has been there in that position. It is a dimensional portal. It connects directly to Orion. When your film Stargate was inspired it was channeled as a pre curser for you recognizing the reality of this particular sacred site. There are many discoveries on your time frame that are ready to happen regarding the great pyramid at Giza. The Annunaki had a hand in building it and the stones were lifted with sound technology. The workers were channeling the Annunaki as this happened. The more of you that gather around the great pyramid in your merkabas the faster the transition will be for your consciousness to open up to being able to see the beings that are stationed around Giza. You do not

have to be there physically although there will be a yearning to be there. This is why it is important for you to open your merkabas and connect in meditation to the first of the Earth merkabas at Giza.

The next most potent part of your sacred sites on your Earth plane is **The Dome of the Rock in Jerusalem** – This is a point of much conflict over the centuries, much claiming and reclaiming. It will be used in political maneuvering to enflame and try to escalate a war on your Earth plane. It is the most religiously sensitive place on your Earth plane and although it is volatile and has been volatile this is nothing for you to fear, this is another important place for you to visit in your merkabas to help bring peace to the area. This is a place of great inspiration and there are many different species that are helping awaken mankind through this sensitive spot. It is a place of great epiphany, not just in travelling there physically, but also in opening up your consciousness and relating to the conflict that has happened around this area.

Sedona in Arizona – Is the next point of longing for you to go. There are many beings that live inside the Earth surrounding this area. That have advanced ships that can become invisible and there are many important channeling's that come from this area. This is an important place for opening consciousness. And there are many powerful vortexes in this place of beauty. Many will learn how to channel in this area; many are learning how to channel and many will connect with the star families of their origin here.

Hawaii – Is a portal of the heart. A birthing ground for the understanding of sacred geometry and the powerful, transformative heart intelligence.

Moscow – Is a transitioning place of consciousness and there are many who are awakening right now in this place that are recognizing the manipulation that is happening on the Earth plane and the plans to enslave mankind. Universal language of vibration is being developed here. Many are being inspired and as you communicate through your internet it will be easier and easier to connect to the different sacred places that are of great importance for the coming transition, the wider contact with the Galactic Council.

You do not have to be at a sacred site to help the vibration of the world. But to join in consciousness at these sacred sites will help magnify the energy around the World of love, of enlightenment, of transformation. Will help open your consciousness, and help you tap into the plans of the Galactic Council. This is a beautiful experience the more and more you let go.

When **Atlantis** was thriving, technology overcame spirituality. It became more and more advanced without the proper wisdom to go with that advancement. Now we are overseeing your advancement so your technology goes hand in hand with your spiritual advancement. For both are important but it is your spiritual advancement that is key to bringing this planet to a global civilization where you can coexist peacefully and everyone is cared for. This will only come with a raising of your consciousness. There is much to be done.

New York City – Is another portal for transformation. There are many beings here that are from all over the galaxy and are helping to influence the whole world through this portal. This is not commonly understood as a sacred site however the divine resonance of central park, which influences the consciousness of the whole city, is a divine portal of influence for the whole world. It is a creative hotbed of consciousness and a place that will send out pulses of light the more and more its influence is understood.

Yellowstone National Park – is a massive catalyst for the transformation of consciousness. It will be a key in transforming the world and the compassion of all mankind coming together.

The **Amartha** are beings that dwell in the North Pole and the South Pole. They have developed warmer climates within the mantle of the Earth and regularly fly all over the globe. They have been in contact with many of your governments at what you call top-secret level, sharing information, but have always kept their boundaries through superior technology. They have as much right to be here as you do. The time is coming where they will be open to showing you their part of the world. How they manage to sustain their part of the world through crystal technology and divine portal transference. They are inter-dimensional beings and they are willing to help you set up your inter-dimensional portals on the Earth. Because communication with the many different governments has broken down due to Human corruption, the Amartha are opening up alternative lines of communication. Because the consciousness of mankind is ready for self-governance with open merkabas, the way they are communicating is starting to change. The Amartha ask that you connect in with them using your merkaba. Picturing the Earth inside your merkaba, the North Pole at the top and the South Pole at the bottom will open up your antenna and the lines of communication to them. You will be empowered in this way and given great inspiration about alternative fuel sources and ways to circumvent the current corrupt political paradigm. The more you do this the quicker the transition from this outdated and outmoded form of governance. Their fields of communication have been open since the portal in 2012.

The Ships over **Iceland** helped with the peaceful revolution and the transformation from anxiety, the trap of debt and the corruption of the monetary system. It is a portal of great hope for the world. This is being suppressed, but nothing can suppress the revolution of consciousness. Your evolution is happening dear ones.

Machu Pichu

– is a point of transformation also. There are many forces here from different dimensions who are very helpful and benevolent. However there are also beings of trickery who have not passed the ring pass not. Therefore it is important that if you travel here physically that you purify your vessels before opening to any channeling at this physical place. We do not say these things to instill fear only to raise your awareness of this portal of activity. It is always a good idea to purify your vessel as good spiritual hygiene practice, however it is much more important at this place that you are aware.

As you open your light bodies and raise your consciousness you will still be aware of negativities but they will not affect you, for as you raise your vibration you will be creating a new paradigm on Earth, a paradigm of cooperation, a paradigm of transformation. You will be opening up to the Golden age of mankind. This time your spiritual and technological advances will be in synch. You had a glorious civilization in Atlantis and Lemuria but this time is the most exciting time for mankind, Much more exciting than Atlantis and Lemuria for the simple reason that this time it is spread all over the Earth. This age you will come together as one. You are already on your way. The next step is you opening up.

The Rocky Mountains
- Are a place of great divine resonance. There are inter-dimensional portals here that are helping to influence the surrounding areas. Many ships are stationed here.

The Himalayas
– Have always been associated in your stories with Masters and Monks. For it is a high point of spiritual mastery required to physically stay here. There are many masters that do. It is a very powerful multi dimensional place. There are portals here to different worlds. Physical portals that can be stepped through physically, much like stepping into a mirror. The masters here know how to manipulate time and space and are working quietly towards the evolution of mankind and have been for thousands of years. Many divine Avataric incarnations gather in the Himalayas to connect with the galactic Council and to discuss this time. You can connect with the Masters in the Himalayas. Babaji holds conferences here, teaching many masters. Brings many people into Samadhi, the divine state of meditation for energizing the physical vessel. Bringing the physical vessel to a great state of

longevity, health and transcendence. This is where the stories of the fountain of youth come from, from his application of yoga. He attained divine perfection. You can connect with Babaji with your merkaba in meditation. He offers the secrets of longevity and the divine application of yoga. His only agenda is your well-being and your evolution.

The Christ heart is blossoming on earth right now. The many masters are waking up. As you are reading this book you are moving into your mastery and the recognition that you can do something about the state of affairs on the Earth plane right now. The greatest gift you can give the world is always your own enlightenment, always your own open merkaba, always your own joy and always your own peace. **For the state of any world is always a reflection of the consciousness of its people**. So there is never judgment of any species that are ready to take the next leap in their evolution. The polarity **always** deepens before the breakthrough of mass consciousness change. So in understanding this you have the choice to dive deep into the illusion or to free yourself and create your own illusion. The platform for your illusion changes as your vibration rises. Therefore the most important thing is that you open your merkaba. That you open yourselves in meditation and that you recognize the reality that you have helped create in this lifetime. The more you see things as they really are rather than as your filter system would have you believe they are, with the many different influences that have been in your consciousness, the easier it will be to transition to the state of bliss, continual bliss, divine bliss. You have all the tools you ever need with an open merkaba and we encourage you to work towards the ring pass not as we are eager to work with you physically in the galactic council as well as telepathically.

As the emotional climate changes on your Earth you will see many great advantages. Political systems breaking down, old worn out ideologies crumbling and many people who are in the old consciousness destroying themselves - not able to handle the light. Understand that nothing really dies and those not ready for the new Earth will simply be reincarnated on a different planet. But this planet is ready for its graduation. The graduating classes are over the next fifty years for more and more of your species awakening in readiness for the coming golden age of mankind. As you are coming to your work with the Galactic Council you are ready for the golden age. When we discuss the golden age we are talking about the whole of mankind and the whole of Earth. But the golden age is already here. With the different levels of vibration that are on the Earth plane at the moment you can live in paradise. You can live your utopia. You can live with complete freedom and bliss. It is all a matter of what you tune into, what you give focus to and what you believe can happen. Once you invest in your merkaba, in clearing your filter system as has been discussed and brought to you by Metatron in the Clarion Call and the Healing book your personal Eden awaits you.

You will be inspiring and holding many different circles of light. We encourage you to participate physically in these circles, for you to join telepathically with each other. **Groups of three** and in **Groups of seven** and then expanding beyond this. The numbers of these groups will multiply but initial core group of three and core group of seven are important to begin with in a new group. Once the establishment of the three has been meditating with the Clarion call and the healing book and expands to seven the group is established in that physical place in the World, that geographical point. We encourage you to start a group no matter where you are on the Earth. The first group of this kind was initiated by Metatron in **New York City** and its members have expanded and they will keep expanding. This portal of light is very important for this work. The telepathic connection of each group will magnify the whole and will expand in the different groups all over the globe. This is the preparation, the ground crew ready for the ships landing in the physical as well as communication telepathically. This is important work. Do not underestimate the importance of you beginning a new group of three. For every group of three that multiplies to seven and expands past this will raise their vibration and will anchor the light where they are physically. This will have a magnifying effect on the whole. Your vessels of light are ready and the more preparation you make the smoother your transition will be to your golden light bodies, your fully open merkabas and the life of your dreams. The complete dropping of fear and the camaraderie and brotherly love in your groups and massive expression of compassion towards all mankind is why you volunteered to come to the Earth in a physical incarnation at this time. Your excitement will build, your passion will expand and your mastery will transcend all dimensions with your merkabas. Your initial expansion with the power of three within your groups will build you up and you will experience collective merkaba travel. Always drink pure water before you go into your circles. And allow yourself to be overshadowed by the heavenly hierarchy. Work through the work books and allow yourselves to drop all pre conceived notions of what is to happen other than understanding that your highest excitement and bliss for your true life path, not influenced by your filter system, your genuine divine joy will reveal itself. Your divine epiphanies will be upon you. All that are reading this are ready for this. **You are being infused with divine confidence**. Be bold, be brave and be ready for the synchronicities that will show you the way.

Iceland had many warriors of light helping the situation in their transformation. And the change has ripples that are affecting the world. You are now in a position of great communication electronically and more has been learned by the bulk of mankind in the last ten years of your linear time frame than was learned in the previous ten thousand years. This is no mistake that this is happening at the same time that your spiritual lives are taking a leap in understanding. For as you communicate more and more and you understand that the vibration of your thoughts affects the vibration of your world, the transition will be quickened. This quickening analogy was given to you in the film 'Highlander' in which the characters who are immortal until they are decapitated by each other reach the state ultimately at the end of the film where there is only one left. "There can be only one". This popular film in your collective consciousness was brought to you at the time to give you the concept of oneness for there can be only one and there is only one for all physical emanations are merely mirrors of the broken glass of oneness. And ultimately all beings come home for there is only one. The catalyst for change that happened in Iceland and the peace light that is beaming out to the heavens is there as a beacon of equality and transformation. For there is only one light, there is only one love and it is divine. That one love flows through you all and though you don't have to have the gruesome excitement of decapitation (Laughs) you will all come to the realization of your divinity. However in this game of life at this linear point of time within your creation, coming to an understanding of the vessel, the consciousness that you inhabit right now is very important. For within this change you are able to go in any direction you decide.

The ships over Iceland are still there magnifying the energy in order to inform humanity that there is a different way and it is a way of peace. It is a way of impeccability and it will transform all from the corrupt, self-serving system that is currently in place.

There is a flower of life pattern surrounding the globe, the Christ grid. It is in all of reality but there is a significant pattern surrounding the Earth, the whole globe. And as you connect into this grid wherever you are it will help you connect to the Akashic records and magnify your efficacy as a divine channel. Make no mistake; no matter your opinion of yourself, you are a divine channel. All you have to do is open up that channel in order to bring yourself into the divine state of bliss. It will transform your work completely in this incarnation.

Uluru – in Australia is a divine portal and there are many ships stationed above this divine place. It is a divine transmitter of energy. The Amartha regularly band around this place and communicate with the ships of light that are stationed above it. There have been many physical meetings here of the sub groups of the Galactic Council. Just being around this divine site magnifies your human potential. There is a portal within this rock that can be accessed with advanced technology and is used by the Amartha and many other different civilizations to enter into many of the underground tunnels that are all over this part of the world. There is much that you will learn about the geology of the Earth that is not understood by your geologists - the actual age of your planet, and what it has been used for. Uluru is part of the guiding force of your planets navigation when the Earth merkaba is working. You understand your position in your galaxy from what you have deduced from what you have observed and analyzed. But the Earth is also an inter-dimensional ship that is capable of shifting its position. It has already done this several times. However, as it is just now, not being nurtured by your species, not being respected, not being loved the way it needs to be for the merkaba to be opened once again. The concentration of the Galactic Council and the members of your species ready to assimilate these concepts is of the raising of consciousness of mankind. Your Mother Earth needs your love right now and though the Earth will survive, she wishes you to survive as a species. All she needs to help you is your love.

Here we give you the divine meditation -

It's very important to do this within your groups of three, individually, groups of seven and larger groups also. The more individuals that do this meditation the faster the transition and the easier it will be for you to usher in the golden age of light for all mankind.

Sit in meditation -

Send love down to the core of Mother Earth.

From your Heart connect into Mother Earth deeply. She feels your love. She is a conscious living being. She appreciates your love and sends it back to your heart.

Feel this bubble of beautiful love expanding from your heart as you connect with your divine Mother. She embraces you, she feeds you the love that you need.

At the same time, from your heart, connect into the Christ grid. The flower of life that surrounds the Earth, send the love from your heart up to the Christ

grid.

This magnifies the power of your merkaba. And this energizes the whole of the Earth and all the masters that are on the Earth right now are energizing the grid.

That energy is coming back to your heart and energizing you.

Feel this energy expanding from your heart.

You are in a divine golden bubble of love.

This keeps flowing from Mother Earth and anchors you into the Christ grid around the Earth.

Expanding your power from your heart chakra in the divine golden bubble you are in now.

This expands the power in your groups and individually.

Feel this bliss expanding now.

Feel the love transforming you.

This energy is making your merkaba more effective and bringing you to the divine detachment of the understanding that only love is real and that bliss is the state of creation, of manifestation. The more often you do this meditation the better for all beings on the Earth. This will magnify all your efforts.

Fukushima
– Needs your attention and your love right now. This place in Japan, this geographical point is a warning and a wake up call for the whole of mankind. Mother Earth asks for your help with this right now. You have an opportunity to heal her, to help in the process by recognizing your divine powers of healing and

manifestation. Mother Earth will survive but she gives you this opportunity to help your species survive before the damage that is done is reclaimed. This incident is similar to what happened in Atlantis before she reclaimed that civilization and went through the self-healing process. The more you understand these divine catalysts or warnings, whichever way you wish to approach these words the quicker the wake up call will be for your species.

As your courage grows within your groups you will be inspired to deeper and deeper levels of service. Recognize that service is always your highest delight. So when you are serving the all you are serving yourself. The initial groups of three and seven are divine numbers and they are this way for a reason, for your encouragement, your transformation, your upliftment, and for your recognition of the law of divine compensation. All the laws of the Universe are opening up within your mastery and as you open your DNA, as you let go of all pre conceived ideas of reality you will embrace the Holy Spirit in your life. Testing all this through your chosen deity. The vessel channeling this book's chosen deity and family tradition is Christianity through the Lord Jesus Christ. Yeshua, the greatest medium to have walked the planet, the Son of God, the Saviour, however your personal opinion is of this, if Jesus is your personal saviour then call upon him. Test this work through Jesus, through the Holy Spirit. For **Jesus said "the Kingdom of God is within you"**. These books are showing you how to access that Kingdom of God through your merkaba. Jesus knew this well. No matter your chosen deity, go through your personal family tradition. Whatever makes you feel comfortable. But this is happening and the more you embrace this and connect to the Christ grid, the grid that Jesus was connected to two thousand years ago, that every human that has attained the understanding of their divinity has connected to and all the masters that are here now to transform the World. This is the second coming of Christ. Not only is Jesus reincarnated on the Earth plane but also he is facilitating what he promised to facilitate when he was first here that the Kingdom within becomes the Kingdom without. All who are connected to the Christ grid, all who are true to their faith no matter which faith you have will recognize this message for what it is and will take action within their own lives. Time is changing. The World, as prophesized has become deeply corrupt and with your analogy of Satan as your lower selves is running amuck among humanity and is leading you towards your doom. All will be saved who call upon the name of **Jesus the Christ** and your **chosen deities**, which will open your **Christ heart** and facilitate you walking the path of impeccability. Many have come proclaiming to be the Christ. The Christ comes without a need to proclaim anything. The testing of the Messiah is clear. The proof of the Messiah is the establishment of the Kingdom of God on Earth. You are ready for your Christhood. You are ready to be Christed beings. You are ready to walk forward on the paths of the Christ, of the Buddha with Krishna love. Recognizing Sai Baba. Recognizing that all of humanity will be judged by the fruits of their labour, by their magnification of the internal Kingdom. This is not like a human judgment - this is divine judgment. The testing forces are there surrounding all of humanity. The pure in heart will lead the battle. This is a war that is already won.

It is more accurate to say it is a flowering, for you are ready to flower. Your lights are shining dear ones and we are ready to embrace you. You are ready to clear your energy systems. You are ready to transform all the energy systems on the Earth plane that are defunct, that are faulty and that are corrupt.

You have nothing to fear apart from old habits of self-destruction. Of allowing others to manipulate your energy and lead you down paths of destruction, **Hold firm to the love inside for you are the God force**. All that is required of you has already been stated in the Clarion call and the Healing book for you to bring yourself into the place of initiation to the Golden age, into the new World. Nothing can stop this dear ones. The power is here, the Christ has returned. You are the Christ. Claim your Christhood. Claim your inheritance of divine joy and rely on your helper the Holy Spirit. For God is Omnipresent, Omniscient and Omnipotent therefore there is no place to hide. God is your very consciousness ushering you towards a better life, ushering you towards your power. Encouraging you to use these vessels to their greatest potential. The more that allow this to happen the quicker it will happen all over the world. Your task is not to change the world. It is merely to change yourself and you will be inspired to your mission, which will be great fun, full of joy and full of peace.

There will be universal health care for all in all countries. All beings on your Earth will be taken care of. There is more financial wealth on the Earth than is needed to feed the world a billion times over. There will be a redistribution of the wealth as the consciousness raises all will be taken care of.

The declaration of independence is a very cleverly worded document that was divinely inspired at the time. And the idea of liberty and justice for all is what you are moving forward towards. This is not what is happening right now, far from it. There is a new declaration of independence. Not to proclaim a Sovereign State from a Monarch but to declare all mankind free under God. The ruling force on Earth shall be the source of all life, shall be love, and shall be equanimity and equality. And all that declare this independence do so with allegiance to the Kingdom of God that is within, that all share in its inheritance. There will be fairness in your society, as your consciousness will not let any other suffer, as you understand that when another is suffering, you are suffering, as you are the other, you are all one. You are declaring independence from a corrupt monetary system, from a corrupt media, from a corrupt war machine, a corrupt healthcare system, a corrupt agricultural system and a plan to enslave mankind through many different methods of control and fear mongering. All that declare independence declare allegiance to the Christ within. Declare allegiance to the Holy Spirit. Declare the acceptance of their higher selves as the guiding force for humanity that allow themselves to share in the bounty of joy, peace, prosperity and abundance that the Christ is ushering in.

Put your hand on your heart and repeat this statement –

I declare allegiance to the true source of all

life, to the love that is within, to the truth about all things. To a fair, equal and loving society. I am a divine citizen of the United Galactic Council. I promote peace in all its forms. I accept guidance from my higher self and all that come with unconditional love. My allegiance to the divine force, the Holy Spirit is upon me now and I am free of all systems that would enslave me. I recognize the oneness of all life and embody the Holy virtues that will transform this World completely. I do not judge the past but appreciate the present moment in which the Golden age shall be born through me, and all who are with me. The power of Christ is upon me. I am free.

In repeating this declaration you free yourself from the mental thought forms of tyranny and the lower chakras of humanity. Satan has been overcome and the world is now a fertile place for all good things to grow. Everything that has happened in the run up to this time, the rapture of humanity, can be seen as the manure that is now useful for all the seeds that are being placed within it. Although the manure is still making a stench it will help grow the seeds of love that are being placed within it. All of these old systems shall break down as the new system grows out of these new seeds. And the Mustard seed, the smallest of seeds, shall grow and become the human race. Understanding their race is an understanding of their holy creations.

Do not be perturbed at the happenings still to come. Know that these growing pains are necessary in this new cycle of life, in this new age of mankind and all will benefit.
    Your focus must be on the new systems that are developing and upon your own vessels, your own joy, and your own blessings.

Come drink from the fountain of the water of life. Allow it to nourish you. As part of the plan of the deception of mankind, the satanic enslavement, your physical water has been poisoned. Your pineal glands have been dulled. Purify your water that you drink physically and recognize what has been put in place to dull your magnificence, to stop your brilliance, to hold back your emancipation and enslave you. The water of life we bring you cannot be poisoned for it has been purified through Gods Holy Spirit. Drink of this water now. Bathe in it, shower in it, drink from it deeply, enquire upon it, and test it. Allow yourself to be energized, to be washed free of the schemes of Satan, of any and all entrapment, the snares of the lower chakras. This will balance all your chakras and make every single one effective and not dominant and bring you into equanimity. Nourish your divinity, washing you clean, ready to put on your white robes of purity.

We have ships in the physical that we are ready to gift to your species that are all over the world in every part of the globe. You cannot acquire these gifts until you have fully opened your personal merkabas and overcome the grip of the lower chakras upon your vessels. These ships can travel great distances in the blink of an eye and will begin the new age of your technological understanding.

We encourage you to grow your own organic food and to free yourself as much as possible from having to participate with what others sell you to physically nourish your vessel. Much of what is sold to you is not only nutritionally devoid of goodness it is actively harmful to your vessels. Use your discernment, do your research, demand to know what is in the foods you consume. The responsibility is your own and it is your responsibility to educate your children and those whom you actively feed. Awaken dear ones. Free your vessels.

This is the seventh time we have participated in the transformation of consciousness of a species on the Earth. You have been by far the most entertaining of these species.

We have been communicating with you through crop circles for some time in order to show you the beauty of the Universe. And the intricate Art works that we have given you are to let it slowly dawn on you that these creations are not just from drunken people with planks in the middle of the night (Laughs) although there have been some Humans who have tried to replicate the works that we have shown you (laughs a little harder) they have been quite clumsy in their attempts. But this is a way of gently showing you and letting it gently dawn on you that we are benevolent, we mean you no harm, we love you and wish to help your consciousness expand. We wish to take you with us, to help other planets, to observe other worlds, to be an active part in helping the evolution of the Universe. For the Galactic Council is not a Council in the way that your council would discuss how many times your waste disposal is put out in the month. The Galactic Council is here to help with the evolution of the different growing species that are happening throughout the Universe. And to open up the many different ways we have of learning from each other and connecting and enjoying life for this is what life is for, this is what the beautiful, dynamic process of creation is for. So that source can have a subjective experience of itself in a myriad of different ways. You will be amazed at the diverse species, the beautiful languages, the stunning artwork and the amazing hospitality that awaits you.

We have infinite patience, so you are under no pressure, but we recognize that your consciousness is ready to flower, ready to expand and ready to experience the next level of your understanding and creative power. You must understand we look on you almost as parents look upon their children when they start to walk. It is always a beautiful thing to see a child taking its first steps. And you do not want to see the child fall. You nurture the child, encourage them and give them confidence to move forward. We recognize you are just taking your first steps into the wider Galactic family. Recognizing what is around you. We care for you deeply and will nurture each one that takes their first steps. For soon you will be running dear ones and enjoying the playground of the Universe.

We have an expansion download for you. But this will only be effective once you have assimilated the downloads from the healing book. This is a portal transference implant that is totally optional and completely harmless. Once you have accepted this implant into your consciousness you will be able to connect with Orion much easier with your consciousness. It is a program much like your Facebook but for beings on Orion and many are open to you connecting in order to learn more about our civilization. There are beings here who evolved on Earth also so are ahead of the class from you so to speak but from the same school, the same graduating experience. Although every leap in consciousness is different for each different species have their particular traits. There are many beings from three of the different graduations from Earth that will be happy to share with you as you assimilate this download implant.

Sit in a quiet position

Go into prayer pose

And give your permission for this to happen

There will be no discomfort

You can turn this program off whenever you wish. Much like logging out of Facebook.

There are many different beings that wish to contribute to this book. We had to be very discerning so you are not overwhelmed. The channel chosen that is downloading this right now is seeing for the first time the collection of beings in the Galactic Council on Orion. As this is all being recorded we shall detach our vibration for a few minutes in order to let Robbie explain what it is that he is seeing.

"Thank you Bashanthi (laughs nervously) it is actually quite beautiful. There is a, what looks like a... ballroom, massive big place. It looks like something out of Star Wars and there's... lots of... different beings with different shaped heads that are em, it looks (Laughs) very happy... to see me... laughs.. em...(Coughs)... it's emm... quite overwhelming... but I can feel the energy of benevolence... err with these people, beings, em... ahh... I erm... I don't quite know what the etiquette is here... (Laughs) this has never happened to me in a channeling before...emmm... its nice to meet you... there's a chap that looks like a big fish (Laughs) but that has legs... and em... well they all have legs but there's a chap hovering that doesn't have legs em that's wearing a top hat... And there's a purple being, very tall, looks like the singing wifey from the fifth element... the place is really big, it's massive it's like... Like the size of a football stadium and there's a big glass dome at the top and I can see... through there it looks like the em... there's a planet that looks really really big and looks really green and looks like Earth looks but not like Earth like the same similar colours to Earth but not like it's the shapes of the land masses are different... there's just an overwhelming feeling of benevolence... (laughs)... I feel drunk, I don't even drink (Laughs)... and I feel like I'm standing in this place... I know I'm in my office but I feel like I'm standing in this place and they are all surrounding me like being very inquisitive and emm... They are looking very humble but also there's a chap with a big trunk, like an Elephant trunk (Laughs) and there is aaaa... chap that looks like a Tiger... like all these different people, they are like people not like ... I don't want to be disrespectful but they look like animals but they don't look wild they look like they are evolved em (Laughs) ... I'm starting to... its like I'm losing the vision now... it's like I felt like I was standing in the place but I feel like it's been taken back now so erm... Thank you for that experience Bashanthi... That was really... very cool (Laughs)... I can't stop laughing now (laughs) ... I feel like I'm full of cosmic energy... thank you for that. That was... very powerful!"

The more of you that open up your merkabas fully, the easier will be the transition for the Earth, the more full members we have on the Galactic Council, the greater the joy will become on the Earth plane. There are many spiritual teachers who espouse joy, love, just get happy. This is the greatest spiritual teaching on the Earth for when mankind realizes that in happiness all things are born. In bliss, everything is manifested; you will manifest the world that you want to have rather than the world that you have allowed your consciousness to create in its present state. You are allowing yourself to be dominated by the few instead of taking on your own autonomy which is the next stage for mankind to open your merkabas fully, to recognize that you have a merkaba, to understand what that is and to walk fully into your power.

The Galactic Council is the next stage in you understanding that you as a species have evolved. But it could have been any other line of animals and it has been many other times on many different planets. The diverse species that are interested in meeting you will let you see how ridiculous your judging of each other within your own species is, for to join the Galactic Council is to be truly cosmopolitan. You cannot fully understand that word until you are in the Galactic Council. But you will dear ones.

The one who is channeling this book has felt his first taste of cosmic, transcendental bi location to Orion. And he took a little while to adjust to this but all that are reading this book can come here and can meet all the beings that he met. There are many different sittings of the Galactic Council and you would have to be in meditation all the time to meet all the members in a single lifetime. This is how vast and diverse the Galactic Council is.

As you sit in your groups of three, groups of seven and more, the more you concentrate on the meditations you have been given in the Clarion Call and the downloads in the Healing Book, the easier will be your transition and the quicker we can give you your ships of light.

There is nothing wrong with being excited about flying in a space ship but your own particular vessel must be taken care of first. For the initial expansion into Galactic living has to be done on a soul level first. We are gently and gradually introducing the physical ships onto your Earth plane that we are gifting you. You have to be ready for this. This message will be spread more and more to the ones who are ready to make the effort and the ones who are not ready to make the effort, the ones who are stuck in their three dimensional consciousness must be left to their own karmic choices and demise. For that is their choice. The Earth is ascending dear ones and we are nurturing each and every one of you but it is time for a choice for mankind to go within in order to see the truth without. The Earth that you are ready to create is a Utopia and the choice is upon you.

The blue lights over Phoenix and many mass sightings that have happened lately will be happening more and more frequently and are serving to bring you into your realization of the truth of extra terrestrial life forms. We are making it increasingly obvious, more and more. And your social networking with the technological change over the last ten years has brought you into a place of being an observational society. You are observing each other and you do this with humor and you come together with your common sense. Your misinformation on your Internet serves a great purpose for it is better that those who are still sleeping and ignorant of this truth remain ignorant for it will be too overwhelming for them until they are awakened fully. Therefore do not fight against the system for it is in place for a reason. There are subtle effects of the ring pass not that are perfect for your evolution as a species. For it is only when you are able as a collective to accept the truth that there will be mass landings in full sight of all. Until then your individual vessels must be worked upon. There will be many that have their own ships that will travel the Universe long before the rest of Humanity have awakened to this truth. It is given to you in your science fiction as the prime directive. More and more are recognizing this as a truth rather than as a wonderful exaggerated fiction.

As you awaken your pure consciousness, coming to an understanding of your merkaba without the use of artificial stimulants or mind altering substances you will be brought forward much quicker than those who transcend the dimensions with the use of artificial additives. For the high that you can attain and the places that you can go within your consciousness are much more powerful than anything that you can gain from any chemical enhancement. As you connect to the higher and higher dimensions you will be able to do this consciously and the differing levels of bliss that you allow within your vessel, within your experience will bring you to a greater understanding of the expansion of your light bodies. If you follow to the letter the Clarion Call, your linear time frame of achieving ascension will be very quick.

Cape Town, South Africa – Is surrounded by ships of light and is a point of great focus for a great souls ascension who

overcame great adversity and was what you call a mahatma, a mighty soul. And in his ascension he is helping in the emancipation of the apartheid of this wonderful place. His legacy was to bring attention to the apartheid in **Palestine**. These two places need your focus right now as this is a great point of you coming to the understanding of what is needed to pass the ring pass not. What has been used as a weapon of misinformation to mislead the World by misusing the words **Anti-Semitic** in order to manipulate the World is a point that **needs to be pondered** and the fear of this misuse and leverage of guilt upon the World to further the aims and ends of those who would enslave the World through misuse of the Holy name and misrepresentation of that which must remain Holy is now coming to an end with the beings of light that will only stand for the truth. **The truth of this manipulation will set you free dear ones.** This situation will come to an end. For the kingdom of God is within all beings and those who have used the holy name for maniacal and despotic aims shall understand what karmic retribution is as the World comes together in unity and the brotherhood of man is accepted and the kingdom of God is finally established on the Earth. Righteousness rather than self-righteousness will prevail and your World will come to peace. And those whose aims are to enslave mankind shall understand that the wrath of God and the fire and brimstone that has been used to manipulate and keep mankind in fear shall be transcended and the dove of peace and the love of God shall prevail. All chains are being broken. All entrapment and enslavement plans are being destroyed and the illuminati of the lower chakras are being dispersed. You are free dear ones. You are being given the keys to the kingdom. It is your choice whether to walk into that freedom and embrace the utopia that is before you or to allow yourselves to be manipulated. The rising tide will lift all boats. And those whose plans were to drown mankind shall themselves be drowned. The analogy of Noah and the boat that saved mankind is once again upon you. Your merkaba is your ark. It is time to board dear ones.

Through facing that which you fear you will come to truth. Through facing the dark you will come to light. All is one in this illusion of consciousness but as you are a transcending consciousness you are open to the old as well as the new. Recognizing that the new is where all mankind is heading, where you will be better served, where your families will be better served, where the World will be better served and where your Children will be better served, you will come into your power.

Understanding the nature of this illusion will free you. Do not judge those that are gripped by the dark. As you are reading this you are ready to transcend that lower part of yourself. But those that are gripped by the dark are merely a younger version of your self. As you are growing up you are ready. You do not judge your young self for the mistakes you have made. Do not judge others for the mistakes they are making. The saying you cannot put an old head on young shoulders is true and from a soul perspective, as you are reading this material, you have that old head, no matter what physical age you are, do not judge your young self. The next stage in your understanding is about the rejuvenation of the body. Although you cannot put an old head on young shoulders, you can rejuvenate the body so that it appears to be on young shoulders (Laughs). We are talking physically and we are talking about the longevity that you all have the ability to experience. You have the ability within these vessels to live many more times that which you are currently living. You have the belief system of three score years and ten (70). Many of you have this belief system. And it is this belief system that has kept this average age for your species. It is only your thought that has created this. Your physical vessels are capable of even ten times the multiplication of this number when you transcend your consciousness. When you fuel your bodies properly, when you take the proper blissful exercise and most importantly when you believe this is possible. Your master Jesus said when you have faith as small as a mustard seed you have the power to move a mountain with only your thought. With a full opening of your merkaba you will understand the nature of reality, that you are made from source energy and you have the power to manipulate this energy in whichever way you choose. As you come into your mastery the first thing to experiment upon with your merkaba's is your own physical vessel, the reversal of your aging process, the ailments that have come upon you through your perceived old age, and the rejuvenation of your vessel. In your linear future once you recognize the truth of your being you will have no need for Hospitals, for Doctors or for healers for you will be your own healers and you will come into your physical perfection and your proper longevity. The aging process is an illusion that you do not have to experience in the way that you are experiencing it right now. Your collective perceived wisdom is to answer for many of the states of dis-ease that are brought upon your vessels. How you fuel your vessel is also very important but once you pass the ring pass not you will feel the compulsion to rejuvenate and people will not believe you are the age that you are when you reach what your society deems as old age. The more you fill your bodies with light and understand how this process needs your input and affects your vessel the happier you will become. And you will transcend the manipulations that are brought upon you in order to sell you products that promise to have the desired effect that opening your merkaba genuinely will have. Freeing yourself from the monetary system of manipulation will affect your being in many different ways and this is one of them as you stop feeding into the negative representations that are foisted upon you in order for companies to make money. This will affect you all and your teaching of these truths once you have discovered the validity of them for yourselves to your children is of utmost importance for these next generations to come out of the fog of manipulation quicker. It will give you the opportunity to see many more generations of your progeny be born and allow you to be a guiding force for a longer time than is currently the Earth plane reality for your species. All thoughts of your demise where you are just now in your linear time frame and what you perceive to be the slowing down of your vessels must be let go of. These perceptions are the only thing that is stopping you from multiplying your perceived longevity. This statement is very important in this book. For where you are right now, no matter how young or old you perceive yourself to be, in your perceived ailments, no matter how destructive and negative you perceive them to be, from this point now make the resolve to embrace the mightiness of your being and reset the timeframe of perception. You are the World, you are a representation of your species and what your species is capable of. This paragraph should be pondered until you have the epiphany that it is designed to evoke. You are free dear ones. In many more ways than you think is possible right now. That thought is being transcended. Allow this truth to settle into your being before continuing.

The many different channels that are spreading the word of this truth are lighting your World up with more light than it has ever seen before. The darkness is failing, the negative is failing but the positive naturally reinforces itself. Each one of you that step into your bravery, into your truth, into opening yourself up to the light, will strengthen the whole. The dark side fights against itself but the light raises all others of light up and into the truth of love. Into the peace that passes understanding, to the higher truth that transcends all things.

No matter where you are on the Earth there is a ship of light nearby. There is nowhere on Earth that we are not close by. With our advanced technology we can make ourselves invisible very easily. Although many of you are seeing ships of light, the timing is not yet right for it to be completely commonplace.

We are helping to bring to your attention the spraying of chemicals into your atmosphere and the weather manipulation programs that have been going on for some time. Although these programs are not purely malevolent, the science behind them is not sufficiently advanced for you to understand what it is that you are doing to yourselves. No one on the Earth plane is escaping this. It is only now with you monitoring all things with your phone cameras that things are becoming much more obvious as to what you are doing to each other. Your world is becoming more and more transparent and this is a wonderful thing for when you bring things out to the light, to the scrutiny of your divine senses you do not make a mistake in your judgment of what is right and wrong with your species. But everything has to be brought out to an open forum for everyone to see what is happening. The more you open your psychic senses the easier this transparency will become. You are wonderful souls ready for the next leap in your understanding, the next leap in your technology, the next leap in your consciousness and the next leap in your acceptance.

When you understand the power of your merkaba and you activate it fully. Not one of you who feels the power of your mighty vessel will feel the need to have a firearm of any kind. You will understand the power of your thought and the futility of these primitive devices. It is much more important that you meditate and you raise your own consciousness and those who you join together with to help bring you into this wider understanding than it is to focus on having guns or not having guns. Having nuclear armaments or not having nuclear armaments for your consciousness is much more powerful than any of these weapons.

The propaganda that is foisted upon you and the evil characters and orchestrated situations of hatred and terror are to manipulate you into fear and to herd you into acceptance of the continuation of war. This once again is purely for economic aims and ends and those who have a vested interest in the continuation of these wars and the manipulation of your mindsets to fear and terror are a very small percentage, not even one percent of your global population benefits from this. The majority of your global population, although held in many different forms of conditioning, belief systems and mass hypnosis through deliberate, immediate forms and past societal, religious and familial forms are all ready to wake up and see the truth for what has been happening. The obvious corruption, secret societies, familial economic hierarchy and some of the negative extra terrestrial influences are all coming into the light. We encourage your scrutiny, we encourage your testing, and we encourage you to use your senses. We encourage you to seek the truth for the truth shall always come out in the end. No matter what secret society has held down their aims. No matter what government has held classified their information. No matter which member of royalty has been protected. No matter how much money those who believe they are above retribution and justice have. The truth shall be known of all these things and the truth shall set you free dear ones.

We encourage your research and now more than at any other time in the history of your species within this batch of your evolution you have access to the whole of human history. You only need look. However we encourage you to meditate upon your inner truth in order to sift through the deliberate misinformation that is placed there to keep you ignorant, to keep you oppressed, to keep you in the dark as to what is happening. Once you come out of this fog of deliberate censorship and propaganda there will arise with you initially righteous fire, rage, indignation and disgust at the lengths that your species will go to in order to keep you oppressed. It is important that you do not let this overwhelm you but instead see this as your younger self. For you, as a soul have been at that point of deliberately trying to manipulate and mislead. So forgive yourself and instead of seeking retribution. Trust in the karmic rebalancing of all things and instead of adding to the negative, in adding to that which will weaken your vessel, which will weaken your experience, which will bring you into a negative spiral, instead free yourself and be part of the solution, for **you ARE the solution.** Use this as fuel, use this righteous fire as fuel for your mission and your mission is always to be light, to be in fun, to laugh at the children who are playing negative games with each other, manipulating and allowing themselves to be manipulated for it is at this point of epiphany within your experience that you are ready to **Pass the ring pass not**. It is this point that you are ready to be cleansed and clear and open in your merkaba and ready to be a full member of the Galactic Council.

We give you another download

It is the Buddhic detachment and acceptance download. It will help you when you come to this point in your understanding of the reality of these truths we place before you.

Sit in prayer position

Accept this download

Once you have fully assimilated this into your being it will be much easier to walk the path of detachment and to walk without judgment amongst those whose agenda is very dark without judging any of the things that they are doing with a full acceptance of their necessity as catalysts for the next stage of your species evolution. You can access this download at any time. It will be needed the deeper you move into your mission.

It is in coming out of the fog of delusion, influence and manipulation that you will truly come into your power. Take all sources that have been laid before you and scrutinize them no matter where they are from. Scrutinize your parents belief systems. Scrutinize your Families values. Scrutinize your Governments values. Scrutinize your religion. Scrutinize the history that you have been told and come to the truth within yourself. You are beings of infinite potential. In your present form the majority of you are sleeping. Even in what you consider to be your awakened form, your enlightened form. But you are only small steps away from the epiphanies that will bring you into alignment with your true self. Your research is important; it is valuable. Whenever you are being told not to look at other belief systems, to only believe what you are being told, you are not being respected and your inner light is not being allowed to shine. The validity of any teaching is in what it creates, how much it frees you to be the better version of you. Anything that encourages you to be subservient to the will of that which you are being told exists without being allowed to research it is merely a system of control. Some control systems are put in place for your own good while you are too immature to handle the truth of yourselves. This is why great truths have been spoken to you in parables, analogies and metaphors. But as a species you are ready to awaken to the truth of yourselves and the overwhelming transformation that this will cause and is causing in your society. You are ready to step into your mighty beings dear ones.

 The sword of truth will cut away all falsehood and you are being encouraged to wield it in your lives. With all the sources of information that you have been told to believe in, truth is the only thing that will stand up and that will survive. The Christ is the only thing that will ultimately prevail within your hearts and the Holy Spirit will help you wield the sword of truth in kindness, in gentleness, in meekness, in purity, in laughter and in fun without any fear. Now is the time for you to walk into your light. Now is the time for you to embody that which the Christ beckons you towards. It is time for you to get off your knees; it is time for you to stop being subservient to those who would oppress you. It is time for you to free your mind, your body, and your spirit. It is time for you to become that which God has designed you for.

The children of your Earth must become your greatest priority. For all your actions are teaching your children. You must scrutinize your actions, you must scrutinize your belief systems, and you must scrutinize everything in order to realize what it is that you are teaching your children. For you are teaching your children, you are always teaching your children no matter whose progeny they are. You are shaping the World by every decision that you make and every decision you make is teaching your children. And you are either speeding up the process of your World becoming a utopia or you are hindering it. Your Children, without exception should be allowed to mature fully before anyone who has matured fully should engage with them in any sexual activity. Any and all of this behavior that is being tolerated and in some cases approved of and encouraged through child brides must be stopped. Your behavior, especially in this regard must be impeccable. Your attitudes and laws concerning these issues vary greatly from place to place on your Earth. This is a very serious issue that you must take upon yourself to actively ensure that the children are protected, nurtured and loved. They must be allowed to play. Although it is important to teach your children discipline, it will never help a Childs development by instilling fear upon it through physical, mental or emotional means. And your scrutiny of your parents, grandparents, school system and societal norms must be of the highest importance. Be brave enough to change and the change upon the Earth plane of the readiness for ALL the beings of your species to be part of the Galactic Council shall be complete.

All the statements we ever make are with awareness, without judgment.

The next stage of your World will astound you as you move forward in greater trust of your own spirits. As you come into alignment of the Christ within and as you recognize your own potential. There are many beacons of light that are beginning to fulfill their potential in your humanity. And with your Internet more is being discovered every day about your abilities and your potential. With each other we encourage you to share, share and share the positive things that you see. Share the inspiration, share the joy, and share the feats of wonder physically, mentally, emotionally and spiritually. Share - for the more you share the higher you will be raised up. The more you contribute the more will be given to you. The less you indulge in the negative part of your being the more it will drop off and the easier it will be for your Ascension. Ascension is on many different levels. It is a very simple shift in perception. On some levels it is you fully embodying your complete God self and in other levels it is simply an awareness of what is outmoded, what does not work anymore, what is defunct. We give you the example of your music systems. Within a century your technology has changed so much and your way of listening to music has gone from clumsy, clunky equipment that filled an entire room to being able to have all the works from all of the Artists throughout History in your pocket. You would not wish to go backwards for the convenience it has brought you, the choice, and the range is immense for your enjoyment. Ascension is here for your enjoyment and you are dropping your outmoded videotapes to having live streaming within your consciousness of all things. You do not wish your technology to go backwards. Do not wish your consciousness to go backwards either. The Ascension of societal attitudes has moved forwards in leaps and bounds in a single generation and has moved much further in the last decade since your internet has been introduced. This is going to keep multiplying and multiplying and we are excited to see you flowering, Come into the zero point within yourself and enjoy not taking another's word as gospel but relying on the inner barometer of your heart, the inner barometer of your soul to point you in the direction of where you are meant to be and how you are meant to be living. For as you detach from each other and the dependence of copying each other you will come into your true creativity. For right now your copying of each other keeps you in a programmed mode afraid to move out of the societal norm for fear of ridicule. But when you copy each other from inspiration instead of from fear you multiply the benefits for each other and you maximize your learning processes which leads to creative behaviors that will completely transform the World. Your creative potential is unlimited and as you open up your synapses through connection to your higher source, to the Christ grid. You utilize the full range of your capabilities. Moving from fear to love changes all things. And in this next stage of your understanding you will take your own breath away in the realization of your own magnificence.

The many different pyramids on your Earth have served to connect the many different beings that have grown up on your planet to the Christ grid. Each different consciousness comes to their understanding of this in different ways. That is why there are so many types of pyramid. That is why there are so many different understandings of what the pyramids mean until you are ready as a species to open up to the next stage of your evolution. What seems like an enigma is a clue that is helping point the way. And there will be many more pyramids once you have graduated your class. Everything will be reset once again and the enigma of the pyramids that you have yet to build shall remain long after the Golden Age of mankind has finished. When you take your place where you choose in your linear time frame. As you begin to recognize pyramid power and the magnification and multiplication of your senses, awareness and power that it helps you with you will appreciate the many different benefits you will get from this. Your house design is changing the more awakened you become. The shape of your dwelling and the flow of energy that is within your houses, the colors, the inspiration that it brings but also the metaphysical advantages of including pyramids and spirals within your designs as you are inspired more and more by your true essence will be more in power when you explore these concepts on a deeper level. And when you put into practice what you are being inspired to create.

Right now there is simply no need for you to pollute your atmosphere burning fossil fuels that you believe you must rely upon. The energy that surrounds you, that is within your planet and that is upon your planet is far greater and much safer than you are currently using. Once again it is only economics and the very small percentage of your population that benefit from the current paradigm. They are not only keeping you cold in your winters but are draining your bank account unnecessarily. The technology to change this is already here. With the current projection of your collective mindset and the plans of your lower chakra selves in the oppression of your population it will be fifty years before you are fully free from this boil that needs to be burst. However, with each one of you that joins the Galactic Council, that magnifies your potential and that opens up the new paradigm that frees you from the oppression and the fear dynamic, you shave time off the linear time frame. Raise your voices and come together in your inspiration and transformation.

Your understanding of sound is changing. As you become more and more aware of the vibration of words and the vibration of how they are said. The energy that goes with the word rather than just the word, the combination of words that affect your consciousness in positive and negative ways, you will come into the centre point and realize the value of your Holy books. For there are codes within your Holy books, ALL your Holy books that can raise your vibration and bring you to the place of great manifestation and peace within yourselves. In the beginning was the word. Your consciousness, your conscious awareness opened up with the word, with the expression of the individual self from the whole in consciousness. For all is one dear ones. Everything is a reflection of the oneness. But the individual consciousness is expressed within the word. Having an understanding and healthy respect for this will bring you into the deepest understanding of yourselves. When you recite the Holy name of oneness you bring yourself into alignment with that vibration and you are lifted from your petty and trivial concerns into your magnificent self. We recommend the Gayatri Mantra. We recommend your Lords prayer. We recommend the Holy prayers from whichever religion you come from. From whichever tradition you feel the resonance with. Whichever point you are most comfortable with is the point that will open the Christ heart within you and that will help you open your merkabas. Be mindful of your speech. Not only to each other but to yourselves. Recognize the power of your words. The power of your programming, for this is what words do, they program you. And recognizing that you have autonomy over which words you assimilate within your being will free you to create the life that you wish to have instead of settling for the life that others have used words to create within you. You are an autonomous being of God.

You are Christ incarnate. You are all Christ seed waiting to flower. The more wisely you choose your reading materials the faster your transformation. Choose your reading material wisely but also choose how you express yourself wisely. This is a very powerful key to your transformation. You have the power to affect many others with your words, every individual that you come into contact with when you are being mindful of your speech and discerning in your assimilation of those words you hear. Recognize the patterns of the words you hear from others. Whether they are on a loop of hypnosis from others or whether they are deliberately projecting their words to you or to others. Avoid the beings who are deliberately projecting negative, vitriol, gossip, hatred etc. Actively seek the company of those who use their words wisely in love, in empowerment, in peace. And deliberately project upon those caught in cycles of hypnosis and conditioning, positive messages, positive transformation, positive words. The word is the key to your transformation in its current state. As you transcend the different levels of consciousness and ascend much higher in your evolution, words will be of no importance, as you will communicate on much deeper levels. However at this stage of your species development, recognize, appreciate and utilize your words as effectively and succinctly as you possibly can.

Having fun with your creations is the next stage of your understanding. Though we speak to you about very serious issues on your Earth plane in readiness for you joining the Galactic Council. And these issues need to be addressed by your species as a whole. All of these issues are reflections of your own consciousness. As a collective what is happening in your world will only stay happening in your world when you believe it has to. The joy of your creations is of course partly in addressing the issues. But in creating the new, having fun with your creations, without any fear of anything, understanding the power of your mighty being is the most important point that we need to make to you. For it is this joy, it is this bliss; it is this flow of creation that manifests quickly, that breaks down all barriers and encourages all others to join you. For your species natural state is joy, is creation, is fun. It is an artificial state that you are in through the designs and manipulation of those whose plans upon your planet would be hindered by you being in your natural state of magnificence. These beings have no power when you recognize how powerful you truly are. And when you create in fun and believe in the power of your visualization and actively open your merkaba, your creations will be truly inspirational. And the laughter and fun that you have whilst creating them will be greatly infectious and will inspire others towards their creativity and magnificence.

As you connect more and more to the Annunaki, the true Annunaki, not the Annunaki of myth and fear. Your mental bodies are going to expand greatly. Your third eyes will be more and more effective in the visualization of what you want to create. Your calculating power will be magnified. With a fully open merkaba your genius activated and connected to the Annunaki you will recognize the simplicity and sluggishness of your thoughts in their previously unawakened form. This will instill great confidence in each one of you and will make it much easier for you to plan your route over the next fifty years of your lives, although it is very important for you to be in the moment, this is the only time that there ever is. Your decisions regarding what it is you want to do, how it is you want to behave, where you want to live, who you want to be with and what state you want your society to be in will be much clearer in mental plan form as you open yourself up in this way. There are a myriad of different possibilities for your life and you can be, do and have whatever you wish as masters. Your mental expansion will allow this to become very clear. In coming to the recognition of your zero point with your merkaba, having opened up with the clarion call and assimilated the downloads in the healing book the life you were living previously will seem very juvenile and primitive. The emphasis will shift from your academic institutions from getting diplomas, degrees & doctorates to having working knowledge of all subjects as par for the course of life. Your credentials will be in your vibration and your obvious abilities and will be able to be read instantaneously by the beings that you will be working with in the future. The system of gaining certification has been a valid one up till now before you were ready to expand your mental bodies. But in your awakened and enlightened society your intuition and vibration will be much more valuable. And though you will continue the current paradigm for many years its validity will become obsolete the more of you that expand your mental capabilities and walk forward in your genius. You will be naturally drawn in vibration and synchronicity to those you will be working with anyway. And your contribution to society will be more benevolent rather than motivated by financial gain. All of the Galactic Council that are contributing their vibration to this book are doing so philanthropically. Their benefit is in watching your transformation, enjoying witnessing your emancipation. They are having great fun in the creation of this book with the channel who is experiencing more expanded awareness than he has ever done in his career as a channel so far. This collaboration was chosen long before the channel was born and the map of this happening was created two millennia ago in your linear time frame. This plan is now coming to fruition. With the expansion of your mental body in connection with the Annunaki, projection of your plans in such a way will all come to fruition as you recognize your creative abilities and come into your power as creative beings.

There are many messiahs upon your planet. The messiah is one who has flowered in their consciousness and is ready, open and willing to give themselves over to the emancipation of the Human race in this current batch of your evolution. Your Messiahs are your writers, your poets, your singers, your entertainers, and your comedians. Every different walk of life has your messiahs. As you are reading this you are ready to walk into your own emancipation and becoming the Messiah. Your myth of the Messiah as a single being who will return to emancipate the World is a beautiful and valid story. But all beings are one. All consciousness comes from the one place and so your understanding is changing in this regard. For you have given your innate power over to those who created this story and who kept you waiting instead of flowering in your own consciousness. The time is now, the Messiah is here, and you are being encouraged to embrace the bliss you feel upon recognizing this truth. The cloud the Messiah is descending upon is a digital one and your technology now being wireless and sufficiently advanced for the readiness of both the return of that which you await and yourselves fully embodying this prophecy. All prophecy is the mental connection to the thought form or map that has been created. Recognize the map that you are travelling right now, Ask the Annunaki for a full visualization of this and recognize the benevolence of this plan. How it will benefit mankind and the wider Galaxy when your Earth merkaba is once again ready to be activated so you can use your Earth to travel the many different dimensions and the physical Galaxies within this three dimensional plane.

There is a lock down that is being attempted upon your Global population in many different ways on order to herd you into compliance with the plans that have been put in place in order to control the Global population. Although these plans are not benevolent in nature there are certain points of infrastructure that are important for your world that are being put into place with these plans. You do not need to worry about any of these things at all for your emancipation is much closer than you think. You must have the courage to explore this world. To do your research, to open yourselves up spiritually and take the rock that you have been carrying on your back off so that you may spread your wings and fly. This is a joke; we are not suggesting you have actual rocks on your backs (Laughs). You have much more to rejoice about than to be depressed about. When you are being given misinformation it is deliberately to depress you. You are not being shown joyous headlines; you are not being shown all of the wonderful discoveries that are happening. You are not being shown the wonderful kindnesses that your species benefits from every single day from each other. You are shown this as a tail end to the doom and gloom and negative propaganda that is foisted upon you. Do not worry about this. For the positive, the feats of bravery, the kindnesses and the benevolence are much more widespread than you are being led to believe.

You are being provoked; you are being provoked towards violence. And in this state it is very easy for those who would oppress you, to dominate you. It is important to recognize this provocation for what it is. For civil war is still war and while you engage in it. While you do the bidding of those who are manipulating you. Whether that is serving to further the cause of financial elites or rising up in violence against them with a uniform or without a uniform is still engaging, indulging and participating in a paradigm that is ready to change. Although there has been much great service by those who wear a uniform, believing that they are defending something. This paradigm is no longer the case. Your merkabas are much greater weapons than what is put in your hands in order to kill others. Your merkabas will switch you into the frequency where you do not need to indulge in these things, where you do not need to participate within this paradigm. It will help you change the paradigm so that your Fathers, Sons, Brothers, Daughters, Sisters and Mothers do not have to go to war with a uniform or without a uniform. War will be obsolete in your physical existence. Do not allow yourself to be provoked. Change your frequency, change your vibration and create the world without violence in any of its forms. You are powerful enough to do this already with a simple change of your mindset but when you open your merkaba you will help to bring this change upon the Earth plane and help to influence the whole world. Nobody has to die in this way anymore. Nobody wants to die in this way anymore. This is not a situation that has to continue. Come into alignment with your divine being and teach your Children valuable lessons that will not include violence of any kind.

These lessons of duality have had their place and have been valuable in your evolution, even exciting. But as your population becomes more and more sensitive, more attuned to the wisdom of the heart, your polarities are becoming much more intense and the depression of the physical reality on the Earth plane is becoming more and more apparent. Your population will become more sensitive as a whole. Therefore it is important as you walk into your mastery that you are mindful of the message that you are giving off. Initially as you raise your vibration and you open your merkaba there will be a period where you will be experiencing life from the same perspective as you did previously but with greater powers of influence. In this rebalancing time it will become apparent to you very quickly that your words have much more weight than they once did and that your influence is now far greater. In this rebalancing time it is important to be very observant of your old patterns and the reaction to your actions of others, for it will be a much more intense experience during this process. It will bring you to a place of silence more often as you ponder these reactions and your behavior. This is a wonderful point in your transformation. It is the point where you are ready to spread your wings, the point where you have taken the rock off your back, the point where you are emancipated enough to feel the freedom of flight. And your example will be enough to inspire those around you once you recognize your newfound mastery.

You are a Gardener watering the plants. You are a Shepherd, Shepherding those who are asleep. You are a Teacher in all that you say and all that you do. You are a gift to the world and as you recognize your power you will be shown the golden path ready to travel the universe. Ready to have the physical experience of coming to Orion and participating in the Galactic Council. Do not fear the warmongers or the manipulation and the propaganda. Once you recognize it for what it is, switch it off. Seek the company of your guides, of the Angels, of the higher vibrational beings who are more than happy to befriend you. Switch on the Orion version of facebook. Keep a journal and note down your experiences. Recognize the different states of awareness that you are being brought towards. Actively, consciously connect telepathically in your groups of three to each other, in your groups of seven to each other and within the larger groups that you will establish all over the globe. This emancipation will happen on a grass roots level. There will be nothing official within your laws to help this. You must take it upon yourselves at this time when your freedoms are being taken away from you in the three dimensional experience. Connect with each other, converse with each other, and telepathically link to all that are ready to connect with you. You are ready for this, for this level of connection will help break down the fog that is being very deliberately and artificially manipulated so you cannot see what is happening. You are already free dear ones. There is no fog when you do not listen to the message. You are free. You are not only free but you are ready to fly. And we are excited to see you come to the realization of this.

China
– Is a great place of transformation. Much of the population within this country has surrendered to an open mindset of meditation without even actively meditating. It is where some of the greatest degrees of telepathy are on your planet right now.

There are many ships of light in the yellow mountain range that go within the Earth. And have been using this particular region for many thousands of years to connect with the underground tunnels that lead to several underground cities in this region. There is a group of beings here that has bases on the moon and that observed your species when they first landed there. They did not wish to interfere with you. They have been helping the Children of China in their mindset as they consider them to be the most humble and cooperative. Much of the technology that has come from this region has been gifted from them.

There is no suitable pronunciation in English for these beings but the essence of the word could be described as 'formless'. They are inter-dimensional beings and from their base on the moon they travel to their original dimension.

They have been expanding the people in China's understanding of economics within the Earth game, which is bringing China, in their cooperation with each other, within the next few decades into a position that will help bring the world into a moneyless situation.

It is within the different monetary systems that a massive game is being played. And there are many lessons of duality that have been learned from this. Your planet is still a long way off from being a moneyless global society. However this is where your species is heading.

There are three extra terrestrial races that have not yet passed the ring pass not, who are influencing the global monetary system and are trying to further the plans for the enslavement of mankind through debt. However, although we are observing this and have not interfered with this game. As you come into the recognition of your divine power and emancipate yourself with your merkabas, passing the ring pass not. As a collective you will completely transcend the need for money. And these immature extra terrestrials will not influence your species anymore.

In the time remaining of you having a monetary system we encourage you to play and do not get bogged down with feelings of guilt surrounding money. For it is this guilt that has held you down and has stopped you from embracing fully the great lessons that can be learned from a spiritual perspective on a planet that has this monetary system of value. We will never interfere with your monetary system because we see the scope for the lessons of the soul that can be learned from it being in place at the moment. Even your Illuminati of the lower chakras that has great financial wealth and is orchestrating much of the drama that is happening on your Earth plane. It is merely a reflection of your collective consciousness. It is when you have fully learned the lesson of this system of value. Transcended it and come into your full power that your species will give up this game.

Each one of you can enjoy this game greatly. And the value of money as a learning tool spiritually, once you understand the true worth of yourselves, will be the cause for great hilarity when you come into your full power.

The sensations that are brought upon your bodies with regards to money are very powerful. Your expansion and inflation of your ego when you believe you have more money is very interesting to watch. And is a great key to your species emancipation. For when you fully open your merkaba and you understand the power of your visualizations. Having enough money will never be a consideration. But you will have much greater fun in playing with it than you ever have done before.

We encourage you to dive deep into all the different traditions that you have on the Earth plane. For when you master these traditions and use them from an ascended place, you are able to do much good on the Earth. Rather than just expand your ego in inflation and self-importance. You will see the esoteric value of financial wealth. Many will renounce this paradigm as they ascend into their light bodies and many will dive even deeper into this game. For a master with money in selfless service to the planet having transcendent fun from moment to moment within their being will show the example and will help free many people from the current paradigm that is oppressing many people and is going to be used as a tool for powerful manipulation as leverage to keep you in worry and fear.

We encourage your fasting. There are many different kinds of fasts. We encourage your juice fasting. It is the quickest way, combined with meditation and prayer for you to transcend your consciousness. We encourage your green juice fasting. Not only will you benefit your body greatly by fasting but also it will help bring into balance your mental, emotional and spiritual bodies in your physical vessel. The more you connect to the Galactic Council, the more important it is for you to purify your diet. Initially you should do a one day fast. And during this fast you should chant, pray, exercise with Yoga and meditate. Concentrating on your breath. Concentrating on your merkaba. It will bring you rapidly into your God self. And you will have quick glimpses of what you are capable of. From these one-day fasts, we encourage you to do three-day fasts. Making sure after day three that you break the fast for the first fasts you do. For seeing the change in your vessel, seeing the transformation in the way your body feels. With your body thanking you for the nutrients that you are giving it you will see the contrast that is needed for you to observe before moving forward towards a purely liquid diet. Those of you who are ready to move on from a purely liquid diet to being sustained purely by the love in the atmosphere, the prana, the chi, the life force, whichever way you want to describe this. Are encouraged to document your experiences in truth. We do not encourage anyone to sustain yourself on only prana until you have lived healthily for at least a year in your linear time on liquids. You must have mastered sugar before you should even attempt to go without any physical nourishment, especially water. We do however encourage you to research these things and to document the effect they have on your physical vessel. It is very important in order for your medicinal paradigm on Earth to change. The more of you that document your vegetable juice fastings on the effect it has upon your chronic diseases the quicker the healing paradigm will change upon the Earth plane. You have much to gain from exploring these concepts. You do not have to be breatharian in order to open your merkaba fully. But the more you raise your vibration the harder it will be to sustain the higher vibrations while still indulging in animal products of any kind. No matter what your physical diet at the moment we encourage fasting. One day at a time moving forward in your courage. Moving forward in your realizations and epiphanies of the health benefits that this will bring you. Ponder these words before we move on.

We do not judge you at all for your sexual orientation. The Christ does not judge you at all for your sexual orientation. The only judgment in this regard of karmic rebalancing is in your lack of impeccability when it comes to your children. We encourage you to love who you feel the natural pull to love. Sex in any form that is with love is beneficial. This is all you need to know with regards to this subject. The judgment of yourselves and others in this and any regard does you more harm energetically than any form of sexual contact on a vibrational level. We encourage you to stop meddling in the affairs of others in this regard. The only affairs of others you should meddle in are with regard to the safety of your children - sexually, emotionally and physically.

We encourage you to do yoga asanas. It is a very powerful way of bringing bliss into your body; it is a form of meditation in itself. The more you practice it the more peaceful your life will become. There will come a time when it will be fundamental in the education of your children. This is already beginning. For when you learn this from an early age it is a natural progression to opening your merkaba. No matter how flexible or inflexible you think you are, embrace yoga asanas as a daily practice. You will never regret this.

Each different being on your Earth is capable of rapid expansion in every different way. But not all are ready for this. This is why we tread softly. You are all telepathic and easily affected until you walk into your own autonomy. This is why we encourage your active participation in this process. There is no fixed future for any of you but there are certain fixed points within your future that you will all experience. Not necessarily within this particular incarnation. But every point in your soul journey is mapped out and through the choices you make you bring these fixed points quicker or slower upon your path. The recognition of the importance of your discernment in all things and actively seeking out the divine path will greatly speed up your souls journey. For many of the epiphanies that you will have whilst reading this book, the Clarion Call and the Healing book will ready you for your full expansion in this lifetime. It is only beings that are ready for this material within their soul path that will be reading this. Do not argue the validity of this book. For those who do not see it's worth are not ready to experience cosmic energy. And it is a good thing for them that they dismiss it. The beings that have made it this far in the book and who are ready to take their souls expansion, their evolution seriously and consciously are ready for the next download that we shall give you now. This is a cosmic attunement. It is similar to Reiki, levels one, two and three which was gifted to the world by Archangel Zadkiel of the violet flame. It widens your channel and allows you to hold more cosmic energy in your vessel. We advise you not to assimilate this download until you are committed to not have any animal products within your system. If you do attempt this download with animal products in your system, it will be uncomfortable, and you will not be able to maintain the vibration within your vessel. For those of you who have made this commitment, it will be a very blissful experience. We recommend you juice fast before you take this upon yourself.

Relax and sit in prayer pose

Accept this download

We recommend that after you have assimilated this that you juice fast for at least a couple of days. This is bringing your vessel to a different level of bliss. You will be more prone to silence for the next couple of days as you fully assimilate this download. Embrace the peace that this brings you. Your will shall become stronger after full assimilation of this download. It will be easier to clearly see the choices you are making and when others are trying to take energy from you. With the flow of cosmic energy you will not feel depleted when others are deliberately trying to take this cosmic energy. Instead you will be able to affect their third eye in a positive way by being in their presence. But your discernment will become much greater in how you direct this energy. We strongly urge you to draw a line in the sand regarding the consumption of any animal products so you can maintain this vibration.

This is the first level of bliss that will lead to your awareness of experiencing yourself embodying the cosmic Christ. There are many different levels of expansion before you reach the Godhead within this journey of evolution. This level will mean a great expansion of your light body. With full anchoring and activation of the cosmic strands of your D,N,A. You will feel this within your hands, your feet and your heart. And your whole chakra system will expand into a golden ball of light, a golden ball of love. In fully assimilating this download your aura will become golden and you halo will be very apparent to those with expanded vision. It is much easier for you, after full assimilation of this to be picked up for a ride in a spaceship.

Malta
– Is a place of great divine transformation. And there are many ships stationed here permanently. As it is a central point for much of what is happening in this half of the globe. It is the entrance point for many of the underground cities that are below the Mediterranean. There is a powerful beam of light here that is an inter-dimensional portal that can access every different part of your Earth. The new sittings of the Galactic Council in this batch of Humanity will be inaugurated here. And all groups of three, seven and more will be connecting dynamically to this portal of light.

We encourage the drawing of Yantra's, the drawing of the circles of the flower of life, the flower of life pattern and Metatrons cube within it, for your focus and concentration and to help you with your meditation. Coloring in Metatrons cube and the kabalistic tree of life within the flower of life will bring you into the focused understanding energetically of your divinity, your power to create within this paradigm of existence. This is not the only physical existence. But all physical Universes are created within the flower of life paradigm. And connecting to the flower of life and Metatrons cube within your merkaba, you will be able to visit these different physical Universes. The more open you become to your cosmic energy and the more disciplined you become about your indulgences of the lower chakras mentally, emotionally and physically within your consumption in all three bodies the more mastery you will have over the control of your merkaba and the more expanded your aura will become. The Annunaki did not originate in this physical Universe but this is where they now reside. And they are pleased to help you in the expansion of your mental bodies.

The solar winds - Which you call the Aurora and Australis Borealis, are beautiful sights in your atmosphere. We encourage you to witness them. For although they are a beautiful spectacle in your atmosphere that is not all. When you witness them physically you can absorb cosmic energy through the weak point that they show you and if you meditate while it is happening above your head. Actively sending energy to the energy patterns you see, you will be able to connect more easily with the Amartha. And they are offering you the opportunity from this point to connect with them on a physical level also.

Los Angeles – Is a place with many extra terrestrial beings that have chosen to assimilate into your culture in the physical. Much of what your culture will become in the coming thousand years shall originate from this place. It is no mistake that the hotbed of your entertainment industry is in this location. And many advanced beings are influencing the work that is coming from this place. The creative mindset of the planet is located here and the excitement of even the word 'Hollywood' is in your consciousness for a reason. Pay attention dear ones for those who are reading this book and who make it to the end are here with a specific mission to deliberately and consciously help expand the consciousness of the Human race. Much of what you need to know for your individual missions is embedded within the films that you are excited about viewing. All forms of communication are valid and when the whole world is ready for a message that will affect the consciousness of the whole without their conscious awareness in order to respect their individual time boundary. It is Film that is the chosen medium. Not all that is within your media is propaganda. And much of what is very valuable and subtly transforming is being given to your species in this way. For those who would never consciously pick up a spiritual book shall still imbibe the spiritual lesson that is needed for them to be incarnated here once this level of ascension is complete on your Planet. We wish you all to ascend dear ones but that will not be the case. As you are reading this material you are within the dynamic vibration range of those that will.

Within your groups of three, seven and beyond we actively encourage your writing. We encourage you to sit with a blank screen and allow yourself to be overshadowed. No matter the form that this takes. We encourage you to connect to your hearts and love the void in front of you as you allow yourself to be overshadowed. If you begin slowly you will quickly expand in your courage the more you recognize the muse that is being put before you. The more active, divine, conscious writings that are put on your Planet, the quicker the transition will be for your species. Begin with small things. Poetry, short stories, jokes. Follow the muse of your heart, the muse of your soul. Set yourself a time every day to do this, the more disciplined you are the quicker you will build your body of works. For those of you whose missions are to expand in this way and whose highest excitement is a career in writing, we encourage your discipline in this regard. For those of you who do not have this as an aspiration we still encourage your writing for it will bring you into communication on a more tangible level as you see it with your guides, the angels, your higher self and the Galactic Council. The more effort you put in the easier it will be and the gentler the flow of inspiration will become.

Peter Pan – Is one of these channeled works. We encourage you to watch it. We encourage you to watch it with your children. We encourage you to read it to your children.

All writing that is inspired is beneficial if you are connecting yourself to the highest source. The source of all life has a myriad of different ways of explaining itself. You are the source of all life. You are an explanation of what source is. You are source. But with the layers of illusion that have been built around you in order to create the illusion that you see. It has brought you to the place of you believing in the illusion. Therefore in order for you to connect with who you truly are you must connect to the highest and purest source that runs through all beings, devoid of all ego. In doing this you connect to that which will be your highest expression of writing. For there are many other beings that would work through you that are on the same level of evolution that you are on. And there is nothing wrong with this in and of itself but you would be just as well having a conversation with your friends. That is a matter of opinion of people who are the same level of consciousness. This will not benefit you being overshadowed. We suggest you connect into the Christ or the highest expression of your own personal tradition. Your own personal familial religion or who resonates with you most. In doing this you will connect to the Christ grid and you will be overshadowed with the highest expression of yourself. In this way it will be easier to connect with the Galactic Council and your highest guides. You will know you have been overshadowed when you see a complete work without you having had to use any of your mental powers in order to create it. The works simply seem to appear from nowhere. The more you allow yourself to be overshadowed and the deeper you go, you will come into the trance state of the adept. From this place the heavenly hierarchy, the Masters, the Angels, the highest expressions of life that will benefit your species will work through you. This is one of the most beneficial points of calling in Humanity for it will help steer Humanity to the next level of their understanding. All stories you channel will have hidden depth and the more you allow this process the easier it will become. For best results we suggest you juice fast, master cleanse as you begin to go deeper. As you get the hang of this and begin to trust your inner self, keep doing more and more personal channelings for yourself. Record them then transcribe them and in this way you will come to the most profound understanding of yourself. You will find yourself speaking great truths and what it is you need to know for your own souls journey.

Karmic contracts, important meetings, preparation and sometimes who you have been in past lives. What you have to do in this lifetime because of the preparation that you have made in those past lives shall be shown to you.

In your groups of three, seven and beyond it is important that you have one power bearer that allows the energy to flow through them in order for it to be grounded in the other two, the other six or more. For the most beneficial of the sessions in your groups we recommend you juice fast. At least for the whole day until the session is over. And to see as part of your mission to transition in your groups in the different levels of your fuelling. Initially giving up meat products. Then animal products, being Vegan, then raw vegan, then liquidarian and finally breatharian as you ramp up the amount of cosmic energy that you are taking into your vessels. It is important not to fool yourself that you can go faster in the stages when you are not purifying your thought, meditating, praying and actively bringing upon yourself cosmic energy through your vessel. If you do this too quickly and you have not made the appropriate adjustments to your diet it will be a very intense experience and you will not be grounding the energy properly. You may feel very profound shaking. Not being able to sleep. Being overwhelmed within your consciousness. You will find yourself wishing you had not started this process without understanding the steps that you need to take before accepting this cosmic energy fully within your vessel. To maintain this high vibration and to actively be nourished by the prana will bring all the energy that you need. And if you make the appropriate preparations you will find yourself moving forward towards Avataric state very quickly. If you are impeccable in your preparations the results will be magnificent. We shall go into this process deeper in the second book. For now it is sufficient that you ponder these words and you experiment with your diet.

India – Is one of the most powerful places of divine spirituality on your Earth plane. And because of the dense population and the wide variety of spiritual beliefs, understanding and participation of Ascended Masters, Avatars and inter-dimensional portals of light, it is the ideal place for the third incarnation of Sai Baba – Prema Sai is ready to be incarnated and will come into his vessel fully awake with an understanding of his divine mission and he will begin after his first cycle on his seventh birthday. We encourage you to link in with him in your groups of three, seven and beyond. For even now before his physical incarnation, he sits in the Galactic Council helping to prepare you for the challenges to come where the polarities will increase and in mankind's transition, those stuck in their lower chakras, or the dark side, the demons of your mindset, the illuminati, the negative side of you that is being cleansed. Whichever way you wish to quantify what is happening right now. Is rising up in full manipulation and negativity. For it knows that its end time is near and these last ditch attempts to control your populace. To scare you, to trap you and ensnare you in your personal experience will only be as influential upon you as you choose. Walk into your mastery fully; open your merkaba, doing the exercises that we have advised in the Clarion call, the Healing book and now the Galactic Council books. If you fully connect with impeccable integrity, these things will not affect you at all. To what degree you wish to dive into the duality and play the roles of the dark beings in this drama will be up to you as a species. As you are reading this, your concern should be only to have fun within this drama and not allow yourself to fall into the patterns of fear. The time is now dear ones for your active, conscious and immediate participation in your emancipation. And why you have been led to the literature that you have been drawn to in this incarnation is becoming more and more apparent. For your preparation, the Clarion Call is all you need to know. The Healing book and the Galactic Council books are important for your full expansion. Be brave dear ones. These books are not merely to bring you into a calm place of being to recognize your divinity in a gentle way and make you feel better about your situation, your life. These books are to bring you into a full expansion of your light body on a very tangible level. On a very profound level and on a level that will completely change your life, and all the circumstances of your life if you choose to read them with courage and determination to be all that you can be within this incarnation. You are ready for this.

Your incredulity at all these concepts will fade when you test these theories out. We do not ask for blind faith. We do not tell you what to believe. We merely present the truth to you and we challenge you to discover these things for yourself. If you keep an open mind and you allow yourself to challenge what you have been told to believe in. If you have the courage to break the chains of perceived wisdom you will rapidly move forward. And if you put these things into practice you will truly have the life of your dreams and you will be called a master. Our channel made an interesting point today in a conversation he had when he challenged, "What is a master?" There are many different levels of mastery. Mastery, as he put it, is "Getting the hang of things." (Laughs) getting the hang of something (Laughs). Most of you reading this book are masters at using your lavatory (Laughs). You have mastered wiping your bums (laughs). Or at least we hope you have (Laughs). The different levels of mastery in your life increase. The most important things to master to take you to a new level of consciousness are your breath, your exercise, your yoga and your diet. These things will make it easier for you to master your emotions. To a certain degree you have mastered flight on this planet. But your vehicles are primitive and you are ready to be shown greater technology. We challenge you to master yourselves first. And the ones that do will have the whole Universe to explore. (Gentle, cheeky laugh) You will not know which ones have. (Laughs) Once you come on board our ships you will understand that it is only other beings that have come on board our ships who will discuss these things with each other. This will make your borders on your planet non-existent. Your immigration will be a thing of the past. You will have the whole planet to explore and you will have the use of technology that will not be hindered by your war industrial complex servants. It is unfortunate that that is all that your soldiers have become. From being noble warriors with a cause, to being servants of the military industrial complex, employees of a dying trade. Each employee of that dying trade that opens themselves up and realizes that there is no need for this anymore.

That all they are serving is corrupt war mongers whose only agenda is money. Will detach from the nonsense they are being fed and free themselves. You are all free dear ones, you are awakening, coming into your full power. These books are about the most advanced point of mastery you can achieve within a Human vessel in this lifetime. And each one of you is capable of this. Not one of you that reads this material is not capable of breatharianism - of feeding yourselves purely on prana. **Keep an open mind to this concept bearing in mind that over twenty thousand of your Earth children die every day from starvation**. When you master these concepts. When you get the hang of these ideas and put them into practice there will be much less misery on your planet and you will make it a priority to teach your children the truth of their magnificent beings. When you get the hang of your longevity you will be able to be around for a lot longer having mastered these techniques in order to make sure that your planet ascends. And your children, grandchildren, great grandchildren, great great grandchildren etc, etc, etc, are cared for, are loved and nurtured, are taught the values of the heart before being given a curriculum that only serves to further the paymasters on the planet rather than serve true human values. In teaching your children love and kindness above all else, every other practical discipline will fall into place past this point. We encourage you to get the hang of your merkabas. We encourage you to get the hang of the downloads in the healing book. Practice, practice, practice these things. Recognize the mightiness of your being and allow yourself to get the hang of how wonderful you truly are. For source does not make mistakes in your design and you are not using even one percent of you capabilities yet. Get the hang of your third eyes. Get the hang of activating your chakra systems every day with your rainbow colours. For you are split spectrums of light. You are divine white light split into red, orange, yellow, green, blue, indigo and violet. Get the hang of activating these colours every day in your visualizations. When you visualize your green heart chakra if you have a partner, visualize them in the centre of this green covered in pink. If you are without your divine partner, send this pink part of your heart chakra out to the universe to connect with its divine counterpart. Use the meditation in Metatron, this is the Clarion call to help further this so that you connect. Follow the divine synchronicities and you will meet. Get the hang of all these things. You do not have to inflate yourself as the title master. Mastering yourself is much more important than mastering others. Even mastering not inflating yourself with having the title master. For when you realize that all beings are one there will be no inflation and you will have truly mastered the concept of being a master. Getting the hang of it only requires your mindfulness, your active participation and practice, practice, practice. When you get the hang of the merkaba truly you will look upon your previous life as ridiculously simplistic. This is what we challenge you to do. Test these concepts out. We only ask for true faith, enquiry and active participation. You are being freed dear ones in every single way if you take the gauntlet, the challenge we lay before you. Do not settle for anything less than your true magnificence.

There is not one thing that you have to be doing in order to achieve your ascension. You have the basic guidelines from Metatron in the Clarion Call. It is the unleashing of your personal bliss on a worldwide basis that is going to take this planet to the next stage of its evolution. The things we encourage you to do will all release bliss within your vessels.

When we suggest you do yoga asanas, holding these poses will not only make you fit and flexible. They will also release the bliss within your body. They will help your posture, align your chakras and bring you into greater fitness than you ever had. This is to release your bliss. And to do this every day will free you up because when you maintain your vessel in this way you have more focus and have more time within your day. Your energy is less scattered. And when we talk to you about being Vegan and Juicers and Breatharians. This is to release more bliss within your body, your vessel. For when you make the transition first of all from eating dense meat and animal products you release vibrationally everything that is holding down your consciousness that is connected to the old way of being on the Earth plane that is not blissful. That is one of domination and dominion and lack of compassion. Overlooking the obvious slaughter, murder of innocent sentient beings. As the ones that have the control over these beings you have a great responsibility to these souls.

But when you decide to give up eating them, you release bliss within your vessel on several different levels. The next level of cutting animal products completely out of your diet releases more bliss. When you follow a vegan diet you come into the health benefits that are associated with eating properly. When you go raw vegan even more bliss is released and when you juice green vegetables you are drinking liquid sunlight and you release even more bliss within your vessel. You rid your vessel of excess deposits of energy and there is a balance. And in the final stage of breatharianism there will be so much bliss within your vessel that you will not sleep much because of the amount of energy that you will have. And you will have great focus. The bliss is tremendous when you get to this stage. We do not suggest that you play with these ideas; we suggest that you experiment with them. We shall go into more detail of how you do this in the second book.

When we say chase your bliss as far as your work is concerned it is very important for your abundance. For not only are you chasing your passions, the things that you decided to do before you came down here and you being excited about them is the pointer towards how successful you are going to be. Doing whatever it is that brings you bliss in the moment. Bliss is the key to everything. It is the key to ascension on this planet. For when you are in bliss you cannot be in fear. When you are in bliss you are in peace. We say chase your bliss and you say "Yes, but I have to pay the bills" It is in chasing your bliss that you will multiply your earnings. Because when you truly have the courage to be who you really are, the Universe fully supports this. God fully supports your dreams and your excitement. And it is when you are being your authentic self that great prosperity comes to you. Have courage dear ones. Release the bliss in no matter what it is that you are doing within the moment.

We encourage you to raise your kundalini with the downloads in the healing book and to connect with your Twin Flame or soul mate energies. For when you raise your kundalini and free yourself from all the negative concepts around sex, you come into your Tantric bliss. Your Tantric bliss is a very sensual bliss. It is feeling with your whole four-body system. Connected first into your own deep kundalini sensuality coming into the core of yourself and then connecting on a soul level with your divine counterpart. This is such a deep, sensual, blissful experience that it is beyond words and will bring you into some of the most blissful states that you can have on your Earth plane in a physical vessel. This will bring you bliss and it will not bring you any of the complications that can come with your sexual relations as how you 'think' you should behave as a society. It will bring you into the mightiness of your being. It will bring you into your God and Goddess self. It will bring you into your own autonomy, which will release even more bliss. And when you are connected together, with all your chakras and mental bodies aligned. Caressing each others skin. Raising each others sexual energies. Playing with, and teasing each other, enjoying and kissing each other, transforming each other, you will dive deep into the creational energies. And this is a place of being able to fully open your merkabas whilst connecting fully. Being lost in each others four-body system. Being lost in each others flesh. Delighting in each others reactions, devoid of ego. We encourage this, we encourage you to throw away the shackles of perceived wisdom and propriety as far as your sexual relations are concerned. This will release even more bliss and make life more and more exiting.

We encourage your sports and your fitness for the endorphins and the bliss that it releases within your vessels. We encourage you to find the sport that you enjoy doing and participate in it on a regular basis. We encourage your swimming and you going to the gym. We encourage your team sports.

We encourage your Art, your creativity, no matter what form it comes in. Anything that you can get lost in we encourage because it is this bliss, the regular participation in this bliss that will bring you more into your authentic self than you have ever been.

Each individual soul is different and you must not copy another thinking that is what you 'aught' to do. You must follow your own bliss, your own idea of what it is to be blissful. Of what your best case scenario is of your ideal life. For you are capable of more than you think, you are magnificent beings, you are masters, you are divine, and you are creators. You create your own reality from moment to moment. The more you believe in yourselves and your capabilities, the quicker your personal transition will be.

We encourage you to take all of this bliss and put it inside your merkabas, to do the meditations of the Clarion call. For when you open up fully with your merkaba there will be no turning back and you will astound yourself and each other as to what you will achieve. Be brave, be bold, and believe in your own genius. Invest in your habits and unleash the mightiness of yourself.

We do not suggest that this is easy. But if you decide to not let the fear programs work their way into your consciousness and free yourself completely, it is very simple to break out of the negative dominating matrix. Once you recognize programming for what it is and you break yourself free you recognize your magnificent divine potential **it will become very easy**. There are two points that you will be at and you will cross between the two before you finally emancipate yourself. This is called cognitive dissonance, holding two opposing points of view and the psychological stress that is caused because it is a threat to your perceived wisdom, your conditioning, and your negative programming. Be brave dear ones and move past this. Move through this and free yourself for you will move into the most magnificent life. We do not suggest that this is easy but it can be. That is up to yourself and how much you invest in your own emancipation. Upon first glance these concepts seem ridiculous and grandiose. But as you evolve and transform and begin to embody more and more of your magnificent potential you will realize exactly what you are capable of. The most important first steps are to recognize what it is you are being programmed with. This is why we encourage the scrutiny of all things. The next is to experiment. Experiment with your diet, experiment with your meditation, experiment with your breath, your exercise, yoga and bliss.

We are not here to harm you, we are here to free you. And you are ready for this. If you were not ready the quarantine would not have been taken off your planet. We can see when the flowers are ready to bloom dear ones as you can see when you have been cultivating your gardens when the season is ready for the fruits to appear. We know you are ready for these concepts. We know you are ready for this reality. We know you are ready for the next leap in your experience.

The organizational structures that have kept you in ignorance have relied greatly on that ignorance. It has been their main strength. For when any group of people need to keep secrets and tell you it is to protect you it is really to protect themselves from their schemes and plans and from the hierarchy and the families of the hierarchies that are in place on your Earth plane from being prosecuted. Those who believe that they are above the law shall be subject to their own karma. The more you move forward towards a transparent society, the fairer your society will become and the reasons for these secrets being kept will not be there anymore. For when a system is open to proper scrutiny from the whole it comes into alignment with divine justice and your own innate sense of fairness. It is always the minority amongst you that wishes to control the majority and wishes to not be held accountable for their actions. All will be held accountable for their actions for all is coming into the light dear ones. The Christ has returned. The dark consciousness is no longer there once the light is turned on. You are being freed; it is you who are freeing yourselves.

There are many planets in Orion. Many advanced species that have mastered the art of instant teleportation with their physical vessels, without the need for spaceships. There are different levels of mastery of your merkaba. You are only now beginning to open up to the initial uses and the initial mastery in even understanding that you have a merkaba in the first place. This will be a widely accepted understanding the more of you that step into your light body, step into your courage to fully open up.

Planet hopping, or space tourism is a great pastime in Orion. Part of this tourism extends further out, even to your planet. And within this localized Galaxy you are one of the species that are observed through this tourism. Just as you go to observe your marine life or go to the zoo to observe your captive animals. There are many that go to observe you and this transition. Most of who are observing you genuinely wish to help you. But there are some who are just fascinated by your different behaviors and enjoy walking amongst you. It has been part of space tourism for some time for beings to hire a Human body for a while, whilst on your planet, to enjoy interacting with your species, to seduce you, to play with you and many times to help enlighten you to higher cosmic energies. Some of your major cities are a point of real fascination for the royalty of some species who have evolved with a monarchy paradigm. Many of these Kings, Queens and Princes are within your major cities, embracing the human lifestyle within hired human vessels. When we say hired it is not the same as you hiring something on the Earth plane. We just use this word so you understand the concept. Payment for the hiring is generally that the soul who is inhabiting the body and who has reared the body from birth, takes a break from the vessel and explores a different Galaxy. Having the experience of Royalty in many cases. Many of these beings that are holidaying here, leave behind beautiful cosmic imprints upon your planet. And you always benefit from them having been here. In your many different situations, of conflict, many have participated within these drama games of evolution as a point of nostalgia and excitement when their particular species have evolved past the need for any such conflict as a vivid video game, a vivid computer game for those who have that particular interest. The human experience is a very fascinating experience for many species. Particularly this batch of evolution, as you have been extremely entertaining. Once we have sufficient amounts of you physically aboard our ships we intend to give you the opportunity to do some of this space tourism yourself. You will have the opportunity to inhabit vessels of beings from much more advanced civilizations and for the first time the Annunaki are offering the opportunity for you to inhabit their vessel. There are seven of the Annunaki who wish to participate in this experiment of consciousness with regards to space tourism. You are only now sufficiently advanced enough, the ones who have sufficiently opened their merkabas, to participate in this. Once you have experienced this the effects on your vessels shall be monitored. We are expecting this to take these seven individuals to a place where the human race has never been before in any of the batches of your evolution. Those who wish to participate in this experiment with the Annunaki will have to have taken yourself to sufficient mastery. You will have to have gotten the hang of your vessels and your merkabas with discipline. With your acceptance and those that have and that do will be at the cutting edge of consciousness and we anticipate a magnificent hybrid experience. There are already candidates for this but the final seven have not been chosen.

There are many different beings participating in this work. And there are many different thought forms that will manifest themselves through many different filter systems. In other words each different person has a different take on how they communicate telepathically. Now that the worldwide quarantine has been lifted and we are ready to communicate with you physically as well as telepathically, we are giving you this information so that you may clear your vessels, your four-body system. Ready to move out of the realms of telepathic communication mixed with your imagination, influenced by your filter system, into being pure, clear channels and meeting us for the first time physically. It is those who are ready to take the lead in the Earths self-governance. Those who have passed the ring pass not and those who are actively trying to pass the ring pass not who will be taken to the next level and welcomed aboard our ships physically. Our discernment and understanding is far greater than you can imagine and we cannot be fooled into accepting you on board without you being ready. It is important that you do the work for yourselves. This has to be on a voluntary basis. For those that are eager to transform their consciousness and raise their vibration will influence thousands, in some cases millions and some cases even billions, the whole planet will be influenced by your light. Your confidence will be obvious and your abilities will be magnified. And the way you will be received by the world will help greatly in the transition. For on an emotional level all will be affected by you once you pass the ring pass not. Do not worry about the polarizing effect that you will sometimes have.

For peoples reactions are always a reflection of their own consciousness in how they see you. The most important thing is that you stay in your centre and you open yourself up to the communication that you are given. The preparation for this is in the Healing book with the communication download. It is important that you upgrade your systems and come into the peace of your own understanding.

Do not over think the concept of being a breatharian too much. For be assured that each one of you, once you have connected properly and fully to cosmic energy, are able to sustain yourself without any physical sustenance. Divine cosmic energy is much more nourishing than anything that is on the Earth plane. Though we encourage your raw veganism and your liquidarianism for that is where you will get the best nutrients on your Earth plane. And encourage you to eat organic, to drink purified water, to breathe deeply and hold your breath at the top, allowing your blood to be fully oxygenated. Every day we encourage your meditation. And once you have fully opened your merkaba and have connected fully into cosmic energy, your bodies will glow with light. Your physical vessels will come to the ideal weight and you will have boundless energy. You will be able to exercise your vessels fully. You will be able to jog full marathons and swim great distances once you have a proper flow of cosmic energy. Although this seems like an outlandish and crazy concept to you right now, we assure you, you are capable of much greater things than you have ever thought possible. If you jump into just merely stopping eating, before you have taken the proper steps that we will outline. You will cause harm to your vessels and can even physically pass away from this vessel and move your consciousness into the next dimension. Die, or kick the bucket as you say. We do not recommend this for you have much to do. We would rather you were energized properly and took the proper steps.

You are ready for the next download of cosmic energy. We will give you these downloads in packets of three. They will balance you mentally, emotionally and physically. The more you allow them, the easier it will be to assimilate them. For the best effect, we suggest you have no animal products in your body for at least twenty four hours before doing this download as it is very powerful and may cause you discomfort if you have. We recommend, if you do have, please skip this point. Read the text but do not do the download until you have been completely vegan for twenty-four hours.

Sit in prayer position

Be open and receive this download

This will widen your channel further and create a divine ball of cosmic energy surrounding you. You will see the full effects of this after seven days of fully assimilating the download. It is a kind of mental, emotional and physical force field. You will feel it physically. It will help you to not absorb negative energy physically through your emotional and mental bodies. When you hear barbed statements when you are in the company of people who spout vitriolic statements and these, as an Empath, normally affect you emotionally. Which affects your physical vessel. Causing fatigue, tiredness and depression. This will form a barrier around you so you will still be able to send them love but you will not be so affected whilst in their company. This is a very powerful tool, especially if you are in a harsh working or home environment. It is a key to freedom in many ways from the negative effect that others have had on you. And once you fully assimilate this download and you keep your vibration high by not taking any animal products within your vessel, you will notice a difference in the people who generally try to steal energy from you. You will still be able to give them energy but it will be on a voluntary basis rather than having the life sucked out of you by psychic energy vampires. Draining people who use control drama, emotional drama and any other form of energy stealing to extract energy from you. It will greatly help with your mastery and you will find yourself in a lighter mood than you normally have when you leave the company of these people. Once you have felt the power and experienced the evidence of this download working, your mental body will tweak the strength of it to adjust it to whoever's company you are in. And so from this point forward you will not be affected by this problem anymore. Only not taking a vegan diet can affect the efficacy of this download. But that is the only thing that can affect it. Your mental body will strengthen it.

Do not be fooled by those who charge exorbitant amounts to bring you to enlightenment. Your enlightenment does not cost any money. It only takes your active participation and sacrificing your lower self, your open merkaba and your unconditional love. For if you practice opening your merkaba as Metatron has outlined in the Clarion call. You walk in unconditional love and you actively drop the lower side of your nature. Drop the grip of the lower chakras in your four-body system and bring your chakras into alignment. A tremendous amount of energy will flow through your system and you will be a walking catalyst of enlightenment for others. And everyone that is enlightened through your energy will enlighten many others. This will have a knock on effect for the whole of Humanity. Everyone that you come into contact with past this point will see your light.

Be aware of the effect that you have on others and the responsibility that comes with this. Because those who have passed the ring pass not will be harmless and innocent and powerful in their divine innocence. The responsibility of their newfound magnetism is not always apparent. You will become more and more aware of your actions and how they affect others very quickly. Ponder this, ponder everyone who reacts to your energy. Remember that you have made a transition. You have grown, expanded; you have widened your power base. And as you stay in the zero point the easier it will be to adjust your behavior that actively influences those who you are able to help.

We are and have been enjoying the seasons on your planet for quite some time now. We travel very quickly around your planet. Once you have the ships we shall gift you, you will enjoy this freedom also. Initially when you take ownership of your first ship there will be safety controls on board. Training wheels so to speak. Which will mean that the ship will be confined to the Earth for at least a year. During that time you will be able to explore your planet faster than you have ever done before. And it will be a completely different experience travelling for you. You will not have to worry about any border checks or passport control. Or any such officialdom you have had to consider in the past. For as a species you are growing up and having use of these ships will completely change the Earth paradigm. There will not be one of you who takes ownership of a ship without being ready. But those that do will change their life paradigm forever. The first trip off the Earth, before you do any more exploring will be to come physically to the Galactic Council and meet the members in session. So part of this preparation in the way that you may view it can be how you would view your astronaut training. You do not have to worry about the rigorous testing that astronauts need to go through to go into your primitive space vessels. The preparation we give you is more important on a vibrational level although your levels of fitness do need to be taken into consideration. It is important that you train, train, train your physical vessels as well as practice, practice, practice your merkabas. Your breath, adjust your diet and come into the zero point. We have space suits tailor made for your individual vessels for before you have made the transition into breatharianism. And once you have made the transition into breatharianism, the next stage of your light body, past this point in your evolution, when you are living on prana ingested through your breath and the light of the Sun will be when you get to the Cosmically Christed stage. At this point you will not need a spacesuit. You will not even need a spaceship. You will be your own beam of light and you will be able to fly through the atmosphere at the speed of thought, which is instantaneous cosmic travel. There are not many alive within your species that will achieve this point of your evolution in the linear time frame from the publishing of this book. Even those who fulfill their physical potential of longevity within the vessels that are reading this book, however, there are some. And that will depend upon the degree of dedication and commitment you give to the process of your own evolution. Re-read this paragraph and absorb these statements before we move on.

It is important that once you finish reading this book that you ponder each individual concept. Allow your mind to expand and have the courage to expand into your light, into your autonomy, into your fully cosmically powered self. For everyone that reads this book is capable of this transition and the sooner you begin on your personal journey. Opening your merkaba with the Clarion call, doing the downloads of the Healing book and expanding your mental body with the Annunaki. And being ready to take delivery of your own personal space ship, the sooner the world will change. All boundaries are being taken away. We have worked with your governments for some time in secret. And while the quarantine was on your planet this was fine. For it was important not to shock your species. But now there has been a breakdown in communication. Money has overtaken good sense and the corruption and media blackout is what those who think they are in control of your planet wish to continue. But the truth is you are a magnificent species and you are ready to take control of your own world, of your own planet, and of your own borders. You are ready to change the paradigm completely. There are no borders dear ones. Only the illusion you put before yourself. There is no need to be scared. Walk tall and carry an open merkaba. This is the only weapon you will ever need. When you really try to fulfill your potential and commit to who you truly are your cosmic life will open up and your intergalactic life will begin.

There are many programs in the ships that we gift you for creating beautiful patterns on your crops. You can do this on sand also. On dry mud planes and any flat surface. So once you take ownership of your ships you may begin to add to the intricate art works that we have been putting onto your planet. There is a program that we have developed but not yet used on the Earth, which freezes large blocks of water into ice in your oceans. We have been leaving this particular program for when you take ownership of your ships of light so that you can experiment with these. Some of the patterns we have left have been miles wide. The last batch of humans that ascended in this way used this program to create the patterns that you see on the Inca planes. These were done by humans dear ones. We encourage your art works and for those of you on this path who wish to share your art works with the world, this will be a wonderful way to help show the transition. For you may beam an image directly onto your cornfields, your hay fields or even onto your oceans. We have been hesitant to use the program on your oceans for sometimes your primitive water ships can be damaged greatly by things floating on the water. But we think this would be a wonderful way to exhibit your talents close by remote beaches for them to be recorded. You will have great creative fun with your new ships and wonderful adventures.

Once you have made the transition and have taken ownership of your ships. Be ready for great polarity and conflict within your family. For not everyone will understand this new vibration that you have and you wont be able to discuss what is really happening. And you will understand this within your consciousness. And though you will be in contact now and again. Your life will be so exciting and exhilarating and without boundary that you will find your old life rather mundane and only be interested in furthering the human race. Your new family of light will love you unconditionally and you will move into a new type of family unit. Nothing can compare to the life that awaits you so we urge you to **prepare, prepare, prepare.**

The Amartha are eager to work with those who have passed the ring pass not. In their talks with your governments they were beginning to make progress however everything is at lock down now and they are eager to only work with those who have expanded their consciousness from now on. The Amartha have never allowed unlimited access before to their part of the planet. Although some humans have been there and have been labeled as nutcases when they tried to tell their story. The Amartha are part of the Galactic Council. They have been members for some time and once you take ownership of your own ships you will be allowed unlimited access through the borders that they had to put into place. The borders that they have in place are not like your checkpoints. They have very powerful force field technology. But you will be welcomed with open arms. All of the Amartha have passed the ring pass not. You will greatly appreciate their part of the world and how they have looked after it. They will show you how to use crystal technology properly. For you have not even unlocked 1% of the power of your crystals. And you don't even fully understand the significance of the crystal skulls that you have discovered. The Amartha will help you unlock all of this. The information that you find within the crystal skulls will help emancipate your consciousness and help you connect to the masters that created them. The Amartha are what you would consider to be Giants. And only just now are you beginning to discover some of their remains around the earth. Their average height is eight feet tall though they can reach heights of twelve feet. Seven feet, in the Amarthan world is considered short. They have large skulls and they have very large crystal skulls at the front of some of their temples, which are used as portals to their planet of origin, which is in a different dimension. Before they decided to cultivate their part of the world they used to roam freely around the Earth. Enjoying walking in forests, and some of them still vacation in some of your woodland areas. This is where your stories of Bigfoot come from. They enjoy camping just as much as your species do. Although they do not do this very often anymore, for you still indulge in primitive sports such as hunting. And although you have never shot one of them, they do not like to be around when this is happening. They are a very peaceful people, advanced and kind. They are all what you would call big friendly giants. And they wish to befriend the world. More specifically they wish to befriend the humanity that has taken their consciousness past the ring pass not. They see the futility in communicating with your species before it has made the effort to raise its consciousness as this has proved fruitless before but they look forward to meeting the ones that have made the effort.

    They wish to gift the world with advanced water purification techniques and devices that they have developed that very simply transforms ocean water into purified drinking water without the need for complicated processes. They have wanted to do this for some time however the talks on this subject broke down due to the attempt to patent this technology and use it for profit. Once they see your willingness to help yourselves and to expand your consciousness, they will release this technology in an open source way so that all of humanity will benefit from it. Soon much of the technology that they have to share with the world and indeed that the Galactic Council have to share with the world will be shared in this way.

The **Davidians**, from Sirius B, that live in Sedona, have their bases on the Earth in the mountain ranges here. The have been expanding the energy in this area for quite some time. And they are offering trips to Sirius B for those who expand their consciousness in this area, in their physical ships. They are part of the Galactic Council and are offering this to ones who are willing and eager to open their merkaba but have not yet done so in order to serve as inspiration and transformation. They have asked us if we would allow them to give you a Sirius B download. Which is an implant of consciousness that will acclimatize your vessel to their ships before you come on board, ready to travel to Sirius B. There are many planets in this area that they wish to show you. This is entirely optional. We leave this to your own resonance, how you feel about this offer. But if you wish to participate, do so now.

Sit in prayer pose

Cross your legs (lotus or near lotus)

Put your hands on your knees

Put your thumb and first finger together

Change this to your second finger

Continue till your pinky

And back to your first finger

Then come back to prayer pose

They ask that you do this slowly, three times whilst breathing deeply. Holding at the top of your breath with every change in finger position until you get back to prayer pose and then the download will be complete. They ask that when you go to Sedona to meditate and to connect with them. That you do so on a full moon night, for this is when your vessels are at optimum position for boarding their ships. When you do this you will be going through a time portal. Although your trip and your experience will last for three months, you will return to Sedona on the same night of the full moon. And you will be able to use recording devices, as long as they are digital in nature, on your trip. The Davidians thank you in advance for your participation.

Your Tantric freedom is ready to arrive and the effect you will have on your partner will be immense when you are in your zero point. Every touch will become an ecstasy; every thought will be a flowering of passion. You are moving into a new realm of understanding of the effect your four-body system can have on each other. For when you come together with your Twin Flame you form a golden bubble of love together that no other can penetrate. And you penetrate each other deeply, mentally, emotionally, physically and spiritually, your souls connecting as one. You will have a deep connection, from your base chakra, to your crown chakra, with your heart chakras on fire, and the profound safety, and transcendence of the golden bubble that you have together. Initially you will be in the golden bubble together as two halves in the whole. But then you will merge into each other and the golden bubble will be one. This is a deeply profound experience and when you are in this sacred place with your Twin Flame it is not just your sexuality that will open up. Every part of you will flower. Your mental bodies will be brought into alignment. You will recognize the role you have within the male female connection no matter your orientation. You will come into balance within your own male female connection in your merkaba within yourself. And you will link together your joint merkaba as two halves of the same soul. And you will transcend all dimensions. Your emotional body coming to balance and being in the centre place together will bring you into the peace that passes understanding. And will expand your heart chakra more than you thought possible. For in this place you are Mother, Father God. You are creator and creatrix of the universe. Shiva and Shakti, hardness and softness, passionate transcendence, awakened power that will transform you, all aspects of your being for you will be a catalyst for each others growth. If you focus on the zero point, if you focus on God, if you focus on the oneness, whichever way you quantify the all that is. If you focus upon this instead of each other, you will ascend and you will be brought into your full potential. And you will achieve things you never thought possible. Your lovemaking will take your breath away. Your physical vessels will improve in health, in stamina, in power, in fitness and in sensitivity. And your spiritual bodies will join together as one flame. And when you make your focus God, your mission will become apparent. You will work together as a team and you will have an unbreakable bond. Your telepathy will be great, your trust will be complete and your passion will be beyond words. All that can hold you down in any mental thought form will be dissolved and cut away. You will transcend all things together. If you focus on each other, and your ego structures, the opposite of this will happen. And you will pull into a negative spiral. Recognize that you can always turn this around by focusing on God, by focusing on the oneness and by detaching from the importance of your relationship and attaching onto the importance of God, you will be brought together and in this purification you will transcend all boundaries. There will be nothing that you will not be able to accomplish together. This is the most holy of relationships and it is always for a divine purpose that you are being brought together. The only way to be truly with your Twin Flame is to focus only on God, Divinity, the oneness, your merkaba, and your transcendence. If you do this all things will be added unto you.

We are excited that you have come to this stage in your evolution. We are eager to work with you in person and we are showing more and more signs for you to wake up. There is no need for you to fear us ever. As members of the Galactic Council we are all past the ring pass not. When you understand the significance of this you will strive to get there within your consciousness. The extra terrestrial races that have not passed the ring pass not, that are participating on your Earth plane, are those that talk of war, of Galactic conflict, of negativity and fear. Though we ready you to win the war of consciousness and we urge you forward towards purification, transformation and your basic training within the

Clarion call. The only ones you ever have to fight are yourselves. Within your consciousness against your negative thought processes, imprinted, implanted, programmed or otherwise.

The extra terrestrials who have not passed the ring pass not, that are influencing your society will have absolutely no power over you once you rise above these negative concepts, transcend the control of the lower chakras, balance all your chakras and ascend.

The physical conflicts, genocide, corruption, negativity and control are ready to come to an end. You are ready to walk into your might beings dear ones. And our more obvious participation in your world will help you free yourselves more and more from the belief in this tyranny. The belief in your disempowerment and will emancipate you to your full autonomy. No one can make you feel little without your permission dear ones. You just need to realize what you are giving your permission for. Give permission for your world to expand to intergalactic status and you will never look back.

It is time to step up your missions. This book is being released at a very significant time. And your empowerment at this linear time is very important. We encourage you to actively destroy your egos but explore your capabilities. For when you understand your capabilities and you recognize the mightiness of your being you will procrastinate no more. You will be energized by divine nectar that will fall from your pineal gland through you palate, energizing your whole vessel with divine amrita, manna of God. When you get the hang of this you will never look back. The control systems that are currently in place, that are trying to dumb you down more and more by concentrating on the negative aspects of your being, do not wish you to discover this for yourselves. For once you open up to this divine honey and are fuelled in a divine way you will have no need for their products, for their services, for their presence in your lives. It is time for the greatest secret that has been kept from you to be revealed. Your own divinity, your own bliss, your own nectar that will start to flow. And for you to recognize how much more exciting and blissful your lives can be, than the scraps that are presented before you. You are told more and more that you have no option that your governments are in control, that only the people with money are in control and that power is a thing for elites. These falsehoods will die away very quickly once you claim your divine heritage, once you open your merkabas and once you fuel yourself with the only meal that you will ever need.

New Zealand
– Is a place of great awakening and expansion. We have many ships here and have been influencing the population for some time now. There is much divinely inspired literature that has been written and channeled here. And some of the first sightings of the ships that we intend to gift to you will be in New Zealand. Wherever you are right now is the perfect place you are meant to be at this moment and where you long to be is the place where you should be in the future. Always follow your heart. Do not look to where you think you aught to be. Look to where your heart is pulling you. Always use that as your barometer and that will lead you to your ship of light. The Amartha have been influencing New Zealand for some time and have helped much of the filmmaking that has gone on here. They are a very creative race of people. And have loved to help with the divine vortexes in this area. The whole of the New Zealand land mass is a replica of an island on a planet near Sirius B. It was made, created, divinely imprinted upon Mother Earth as a wedding present, a divine bonding ceremony between Queen Alucias and King Abraham of the Abrahamic dynasty of which the Davidians are the direct descendants of. This land mass was created with great love with full cooperation of Mother Earth. It is a place of great divine resonance and many who are drawn here come here because of their past lives on Sirius B and their connection to the Abrahamic dynasty.

We now give you your first initiation ready for you opening the flow of divine nectar from your pineal gland that will begin to drip from your pallet. And you will begin to taste this. This is the first initiation; you will receive the second and third initiation in the second book.

Stand with your legs slightly apart

Put your hands on your heart and put all of your concentration on the centre of your mind. The centre of your brain where your pineal gland is

Picture your pineal gland dripping onto your pallet

And picture your whole body within the Sun

Your local Sun and Betelgeuse is connected now

You are opening up to the power of a billion Suns

All are concentrated upon your pineal gland now

All blocks to your pineal gland are being taken away

You are being placed within the centre of the Suns

You are being energized with a constant drip

Open to receive this

Visualize this constantly dripping into your mouth

You will begin to taste this nectar flowing

This initiation is being guided by

Prema Sai Baba, Sathya Sai Baba and Shirdi Sai Baba

The triple incarnation surrounds you now

And your lips are being silenced while this initiation takes root

Sai Baba blesses your life and your mission and sets you on the straight road - The path of immortality.

Allow this to sink into the very core of your being. This is the most profound initiation that any Human being has ever participated in within this batch of your evolution. Allow yourself time to fully assimilate this.

This initiation will focus your attention on your pineal gland and your connection to all the physical power in the Universe. Once the nectar starts to flow you will not need to take any physical sustenance ever again in this lifetime. And you will taste this in your mouth. You will be fully nourished, fully energized, you will feel like you have eaten and it will nourish your body like it has never been nourished before. Allow this initiation to settle in your being. It may be overwhelming but we urge you to keep drinking water whilst it embeds fully into your consciousness. This is a process that is helped by your opening merkaba. Your physical vessels are changing as you open up to the next step in your evolution. There have been many that have already opened this door. Many are being sustained by divine nectar already. And the process has been widely criticized and denounced as fraud and those who practice it denounced as charlatans. This is a very real process dear ones. Your physical vessels are opening up to the sustenance of the universe. And once you have made the transition and the process is complete, with all three initiations, and you are living on divine nectar, you will wonder how you ever lived without this.

This divine manna gives you every single nutrient you could ever need. And although you may eat and you may drink, this will be a voluntary thing. And it will generally be only to have a different taste in your mouth sporadically. You will always feel better when you are only relying upon the divine nectar that will flow into your mouth.

During the process of assimilation, we encourage your daily yoga, your daily meditation. It is normal to want to sleep during the assimilation of this initiation. During this process you may be overwhelmed. But your body is going through a change. Be kind to yourself and actively take the stress off of yourself through meditation, prayer, yoga asanas and rest.

We encourage you to document this process, to journal it, to put it in your diaries as to how you are feeling. How long it takes to complete the process. For as time moves on and more and more discover this gift we encourage your discussion from those who have completed the process and are completely living on light. For this divine manna is made of light, is made of God, is made of source energy, is the creation of the universe. It is Gods gift to you for the golden age. And you are all worthy of this but not all are ready for this. Those who are reading this are all ready for this initiation or you would not be reading this literature. This is a very special book and each individual that is reading these words is at the point in their evolution where they are ready to experience God feeding them physically, directly. Past the point of the assimilation of these initiations your faith will be complete for you will be being sustained by God at all times. This will magnify all your powers. Your energy will be as it should be. And no matter the ailment, chronic or otherwise, you will come into perfect health. This divine nectar activates all the natural medicine within your vessel. For your physical vessel is a complete natural pharmacy and those who are living on this divine nectar will have no need of any artificial chemicals ever again. Once the wider humanity understand the validity and the efficacy of this process and this divine amrita, there will be no need for the pharmaceutical industry. Therefore be prepared for this process to be maligned, discredited and undermined by those who wish to make a profit from your illness. The time for that paradigm is coming to an end. An industry whose main concern should be your healing and well being unfortunately is more invested in profit. You are free dear ones. Your vessels are capable of so much more than you know. As you are reading this, get ready to be enlightened as to all your capabilities.

We ask you to test these things out. Test all these things out and do not settle for anything less than your own magnificence. You are divine beings dear ones and you are ready for the next stage in your evolution. Being sustained on divine light, being in your integrity, being awakened to your full capabilities, an open merkaba, great longevity, perfect health, abundance, the ability to go anywhere in the world and after you have helped with the transition on the earth to be able to go anywhere in the universe.

The wider humanity is not ready to be sustained on divine nectar, to be breatharians, because they are not ready for galactic travel. It makes perfect sense for you, as you ascend to a new way of being as galactic citizens, part of the Galactic Council, that when you travel that you have no need for fuel, that you have no need to urinate or defecate. There is no real need for toilets aboard your spaceships, however for those who are in the process of the transformation there are facilities on board.

Your world is changing, and you are ready for this change. There is much to do and there is still much to overcome. For your species is fighting a divine war of consciousness in its transformation into the next level of its evolution. For you to participate in this with efficacy and power and bring your people to the next level, all you have to do is open yourselves up. For when you come into your real bliss, once you open your merkabas. Once you fully download and upgrade and make the transition to being fed by divine nectar, you are part of the new humanity. Walking into your Christhood. Ready to love all and serve all.

We leave you with these premises. We urge you to dive deep into this truth. Bathe in the divine nectar of purification.

Open up to the first divine initiation in readiness for the second book, where we will take you into the utopia of being that you are ready to experience.

All is well dear ones.

We are the Galactic Council.

We thank you for your participation.

Be ready.

Your time has come.

Made in the USA
San Bernardino, CA
05 April 2018